More Haunted Michigan

New Encounters with Ghosts of the Great Lakes State

Rev. Gerald S. Hunter

THUNDER BAY
PRESS

West Branch, Michigan

More Haunted Michigan:
New Encounters with Ghosts of the Great Lakes State
by Rev. Gerald S. Hunter

Hunter, Gerald S.

    More Haunted Michigan : new encounters with ghosts of the Great Lakes State / Gerald S. Hunter. — 1st ed.
    p. cm.
    Includes index.
    LCCN: 2002112559
    ISBN 13: 978-1-933-27201-6

    1. Ghosts—Michigan. 2. Haunted places—Michigan.
I. Title.

BF1472.U6H862 2002   133.1'09774
                         QBI02-200817

THUNDER BAY
—— P R E S S ——

Contents

Preface vii
The Ones That Got Away xiii
Foreword xix
Haunt Meter xxiii

1. Now This Is Invasion of Privacy 3
Byron

2. The Ghost of the Grieving Gentleman 19
Dearborn

3. No Help with the Wicked 25
Dearborn Heights

4. Pull up a Chair and Make Yourself
Comfortable / The Gang's All Here 51
Dowagiac

5. Center Stage with the Ghosts 67
Dowagiac

6. The Ghostly Caregiver 77
Escanaba

7. Antique Ghosts 85
Jackson

8. Added Attraction 101
Jackson

9. Hired Help 107
Leslie

10. **The Ghost Who Protects Her Domain** 113
Livonia

11. **The Ghost Who Growls** 125
Mackinac Island

12. **This Cemetery Talks** 133
Manchester

13. **Stay Out of Those Woods** 143
Mid-Michigan

14. **Mirror, Mirror, on the Wall** 151
Midland

15. **Not This House, Thank You** 165
Milford

16. **Eugene** 171
Otsego

17. **Who (or What) Is Causing
All Those Lights?** 177
Watersmeet

18. **Just Who Is This Woman, Anyway?** 185
Westland

19. **A Haunted Dwelling in
the Author's Birthplace!** 191
Ypsilanti

Beyond the State Line

20. **Who Is That Woman
in the Photograph?** 201
Gettysburg, Pennsylvania

21. It's Still Alma's House **209**
New York, New York

22. These Ghosts Are Everywhere **215**
Tombstone, Arizona

23. The River Ghost **221**
Bruceton Mills, West Virginia

Index **225**
About the Author **231**
Publisher's Credits **232**

Preface

ALONG WITH THE ghostly text within my first book, *Haunted Michigan: Recent Encounters with Active Spirits*, was an invitation directed at readers who wished to contact me. The result was a fair amount of letters, and an abundance of re-routed e-mail messages.

As it was not always easy to find time to answer such a copious amount of correspondence, many of my attempts to hook up with these folks were delayed—sometimes far too long—for which I humbly apologize. The tragedy of this is that a good many leads for haunted dwellings to explore were lost, as our society today has become quite mobile, frequently shifting from one locale to another.

Some of the e-mails and letters I received would have developed, I believe, into the most fascinating of stories. Alas, to read an interesting account of someone's personal run-in with spectral beings, and not have the access needed for appropriate follow up, is frustrating. I offer the following story as an example.

The best I can do is tell you that it comes from a young woman named Anjanette and that her tale was spirited my way by e-mail. What little I offer you at this time is intriguing—but it's also akin to being served a scrumptious appetizer at an upscale eatery, only to be denied the main course when the waitstaff ignores the presence of your rumbling stomach. Sadly, Anjanette's e-mail address did not receive my fevered attempts to connect, and the telephone number she had earlier relayed to me had been disconnected. In spite of that, I'll just go ahead and throw you the bone she threw me.

Location of Haunting: A former one-room schoolhouse,

now serving as a private residence. Its location is unknown. However, I believe that with a little bit of detective work, one may come close to discovering its whereabouts. For instance, I was contacted from the "810" area code, which may place the haunted structure somewhere in the geographic area including Macomb, St. Clair, Lapeer, Genesee, and Sanilac Counties, with a little slop over into Oakland and Livingston Counties. As intellectually savvy Michiganders will recognize, this is the area beginning just north of Detroit with the city of Warren and extending northward toward Port Sanilac on the shores of Lake Huron to the east, and Clio/Mt. Morris on the extreme northwest. Also, I would suppose there exists some sort of preservationist society out there dealing with one-room schoolhouses, and since this one was converted into a single-family home, it just might be possible to stumble across it with their help. Happy hunting if you try!

Period of Haunting: From what I managed to gather from the original e-mail, the haunting dates back at least to the very early 1960s and possibly further back than that. It is obvious from her frightening account that the intensity of the haunting continues to this day.

Date of Investigation: No investigation was possible, and all information was gleaned from a solitary e-mail message. *Dang, I wish I had followed up more quickly!*

Description of Place: I have a bit more information here, although nothing precise. The structure was once a one-room schoolhouse, built, as Anjanette points out, in 1856, which would make it one of the oldest original structures still standing in this Wolverine State of ours. She goes on to say it was continuously used as a schoolhouse until the early 1960s, a remarkable tenure for any brick and mortar testament to higher education, let alone a one-room outfit.

The Haunt Meter * * * *
It's rather difficult assigning a score to a haunt I've not

been properly introduced to, but judging purely from
Anjanette's description of events, it sounds like a pretty
frightening place to live, let alone learn the three "R's."

"Just What Sort of Schoolhouse Was This?"

Having read my first book, Anjanette says she was
moved to relate to me a bit of her own haunted history.
It appears that when she married her husband, Steve,
they settled in to the house he had grown up in—a
former one-room schoolhouse—purchasing it not long
after their marriage. She was aware, as she says, that "it
was sort of an open secret that the house was haunted."
Apparently undaunted by such knowledge, she and her
hubby set up housekeeping within its not so hallowed
halls.

It's plenty frightening enough to move into a home
only to discover specters of the dead scurrying about,
but imagine what sort of trepidation would accompany
the foreknowledge that you will soon share your existence with restless spirits. "The house boasted the usual
haunting activities," says Anjanette. "There were doors
opening and shutting without any help, disembodied
footsteps creaking across the floors, and the like. We
bought the place with full knowledge of its otherworldly
inhabitants, and really all was well for us there until we
decided to remodel. It was then, if you'd pardon the
expression, that all hell broke loose."

It is interesting to note how frequently ghosts get
possessively peeved about folks tinkering around with
the decor of the home they had once inhabited in the
flesh, and now inhabit in a more vaporous form. Time
and again people have written to tell me how ghostly
outrage infested their every effort to update and person-
alize their home. In a strange way I guess it's only
logical—if the dead truly are hanging around, it may
well be because they are maladjustedly attached to the
home they insist is still theirs. How would we like it if

some intrusive clod invaded our privacy and started ripping up walls and tearing out flooring?

As for Anjanette and Steve, their ghosts were less than appreciative of their rehabbing efforts, and had no reservations about expressing their outrage. "At night it sounded like someone was bowling with sixty-pound bowling balls in our living room," says Anjanette. And if that weren't a subtle enough hint that conditions had become unacceptable, the ghosts decided a few rude awakenings were in order. "My sister-in-law reported to us one morning that she had the feeling of something very large and menacing looming over her whenever she would spend the night with us." Just exactly what this menacing entity was, I can't tell, as further details were too sketchy.

If the ghosts are less than hospitable to house guests, try to imagine how they felt about the fine folk who held the mortgage. Interrupting their sleep turned out to be even more violent. "Both my husband and myself were awakened from sleep on many occasions by someone pounding on the back door," says Anjanette. "We'd be sound asleep, and all of a sudden the pounding would begin, a really angry sound, and then we'd hear a voice calling out our names. But, of course, upon investigation, there was never anyone there. And the really odd thing was that this pounding and yelling by our unseen visitor did not wake up our dogs, who were kenneled within six feet of the back door."

Anjanette went on to say that there were simply too many frightening experiences to relate in one e-mail, and assured me that she could supply scads of friends and relatives who could relate their own frightening escapades in the house. One such experience dealt with good friends who stopped over for an evening visit.

"We were entertaining our guests," says she, "and the conversation turned to the ghosts we have living with us. One of our guests made some disparaging remark about how there is no such thing as a haunted house, and just as those words left his mouth, the laundry room door swung open. They left in a hot minute!" Apparently, ghosts don't appreciate having their existence questioned, but then again, who does?

I salivate when I think about all the potential stories this house had to offer one who pens ghostly tales for a hobby, but alas, they appear to be lost forever! My only hope is that Anjanette and Steve come across their story in this book, and once again make contact with me. I promise them a speedy reply.

Meanwhile, as this haunted lead evaporates to a mere wisp in the recesses of my hard drive, I leave you with the information that Anjanette and Steve have exited the haunted former schoolhouse, opting for more subdued accommodations. "What sort of settled us on the decision to leave was an incident that was, for me, the most memorable of our stay there," says Anjanette. "I was several months pregnant at the time, and I had gone upstairs for something, although I can't remember right now what it was that I wanted. Anyway, on the way back down the stairs, someone unseen decided to give me a bit of help going down by pushing me. That was it for me, it just started to feel like things were really turning ugly. After the baby was born, we left."

Well, there it is, a terrific story that could have been even better had I followed up with them right away. But they're not the only ones. . .

The Ones That Got Away

I MUST ADMIT I had a great deal of fun prowling about the cities and countryside of Michigan in search of the restless spirits of the dead. I relished prodding my nose into the nooks and crannies of darkened hallways and dank basements, hoping all the while to catch at least a fleeting glimpse of some elusive specter.

For the most part, I am satisfied with my results, and I offer within these pages what I consider to be the most interesting of the haunted places to which I was privy. As satisfied as I am though, I must admit I've tasted the bitter pill of disappointment as well. If I've learned anything at all as a result of my literary efforts, it is that fate is capricious. Some excellent prospects slipped from my grasp for an array of reasons. And now I present some leads which reflect that excellent potential, but which resulted in dead ends when personal contact was attempted.

Soooo, here we go . . .

From Reese, Michigan came the tale of romantic love blossoming into a beautiful honeymoon in Dunvegan, Scotland. What was intended to be a journey of the heart nearly turned into the raising of the hackles when the ghost of MacLeod Castle began to stalk the blushing bride. If that were not enough to add to the sacredness of their nuptials, it seems that the house they purchased in Reese included more than the obligatory thirty-year mortgage, as apparitions tend to peer out the windows, smoky mists waft lazily through the bedrooms, and the family computer and scanner decide to fire themselves up for a session of word processing all their own. **Final Result:** *Lost when e-mail and phone calls produced no contact with the living.*

From New Baltimore, Michigan. I received an e-mail from someone anxious to know why the figure of a man in dungarees hovers in the corner of their basement and sometimes pounds on the basement door in the middle of a good night's sleep. According to the message they sent my way, this fellow has been spotted in the house by scores of friends and relatives. *Final Result: Lost when the e-mail address they used was no longer in operation.*

From Caro, Michigan was a plea for me to visit a home where lights flash on and off for no apparent reason and footsteps are heard treading the hardwood floors of this ancient farmhouse. Children are frightened by a woman who drifts through the bathroom while it's in use (a most inopportune time for a cordial visit), and the woman of the house is met with loud banging noises on the walls whenever she admonishes her children for some infraction of family rules. *Final Result: Lost when the e-mail address they supplied was inoperative.*

From Detroit, Michigan. I received an outright and nearly hostile reply to inquiries concerning a famous, upscale restaurant. Several people had notified me of the ghosts who torment the staff, independently operate the elevator, and generally make the kitchen help nervous. One patron even admitted in an e-mail of having seen one of the ghosts in that fine manse. *Final Result: I was told, in no uncertain terms, that my inquiries were not acceptable to the projected image of the eatery. Hmmph!*

From Traverse City, Michigan was a wonderful conversation from someone who attended an historic church that was home to disembodied voices and loud banging noises. My contact in that city of cherries insisted she knew several other parish members in good standing who had actually seen ghostly figures dressed in garb from decades past flitting about the pews. *Final*

Result: *Story lost forever when my lovely contact fumed, "Investigate the church and talk to my pastor!? Don't you dare. If he found out I told you these things, he'd think I was crazy." Hmmm.*

From Royal Oak, Michigan was the tale of one of the oldest homes in that rather upscale community experiencing strange phenomena. Furniture would rearrange itself while the family was out, and odd, pungent odors would inexplicably fill the rooms, driving the family outdoors for several minutes until the air would suddenly freshen itself once again. Perhaps the most disconcerting event, though, were the faces that would show up for no reason on the upstairs bedroom window. **Final Result:** *Mom and kids anxiously approved a full blown story—Dad didn't. He was bigger than me.*

From East Lansing, Michigan came the letter from an employee of a local shoe store, who maintains, in all sincerity, that the shop is host to at least one playful spirit. Shoes taken out to a customer for fitting will suddenly be misplaced, and boxes of footwear will fly off the shelves in the back storeroom, ending up in a mixed up pile of assorted colors and sizes. At least one customer asked an employee for assistance, only to watch in horror as the person she addressed stride past her and seem to vaporize before reaching the sales counter. **Final Result:** *The manager, who admits the place has some creepy things going on, decided publication of the story might possibly be bad for business. He asked me to back off, and I did.*

From Redford, Michigan arrive the story of a little boy who insists he sees an older man standing in his doorway whenever he is playing alone in his room. Lights go on and off, and, interestingly enough, food prepared for the family's consumption often has a helping or two withdrawn from its contents before they have had a chance to partake. It is rumored that someone committed suicide in the home, and that the restless spirit still roams the rooms, living unseen among the inhabitants. ***Final Result:*** *By the time I had attempted contact with the family, they had moved. Incidentally, when my phone call was answered I just assumed I was speaking with one of the folks who had made contact with me, so I innocently introduced myself and named my reason for calling. The new owners of the home were less than pleased to discover their home may be harboring a ghost or two. Oops!*

From a Grand Rapids Suburb was an account of a single family home where the ghosts toss the freshly laundered clothing out of the washing machine and onto the laundry room floor. They also wait until the house is quiet for the night and turn on the television, making sure the sound is full speed ahead. At least one spirit of an elderly woman has been seen peeking into the bedrooms, supposedly checking up on the children sleeping inside. On one occasion, an occupant was chased down the stairs and out onto the lawn by an angry, foul smelling ghost with rotten teeth, if not to say rotten disposition. ***Final Result:*** *I discovered the lead came to me from a teenaged family member who hadn't secured her parents' permission before writing me. They said they would rather cope with the haunting on their own than run the risk of having "nosy nutcases" milling about the place. I trust they weren't referring to me.*

From Marquette, Michigan came a beauty of a lead. I was sitting in a downtown brew pub with my eldest son Rob, when the waitress noticed we weren't regulars and asked what brought us to Marquette. Over great Reuben sandwiches, we told her we were checking out haunted places, and she really opened up about the ghost she and the staff find themselves tolerating. ***Final Result:*** *The story dissipated like a hot mist on a cold night when* *the owner, a very warm and personable woman, announced that she was completely unaware of any ghost lingering about the brew tanks. I had to take the owner's word, and let this one go.*

Well, there you have it, just some of the places that could have found fame between the covers of this book. There were a good deal more than these that slipped by me, but you get the general idea. All I ask is that you wish me better luck next time.

Foreword

But First, A Few Observations

I WISH TO sincerely thank all the fine folks who helped to make *Haunted Michigan: Recent Encounters with Active Spirits* such a spirited success. You took the chance of shelling out your hard-earned cash on an untried author, and for that I am grateful. It is with that gratitude in mind that I wrote each chapter of this volume about more haunted places in the Great Lakes State.

While I have been involved in a great many inquiries into haunted homes and public structures, I do not consider myself an expert in the field of "ghostology." I have simply followed through on my fascination with ghosts and things that go bump in the night—or the daytime, for that matter. Perhaps that is why I was so surprised to discover that many people assumed I have some sort of professional training in parapsychology (I don't), or that I possess some sort of deep and mystic psychic abilities (I wish I did). I do, however, admit to having had many personal encounters with events that defied any attempt at rational explanation.

Many readers contacted me to ask for help with their haunting. I suppose they were hopeful I could rid their domain of the ghosts who were invasive of their lives and privacy. I have never intended to do such a thing. Who am I to extricate someone from their home if they don't wish to depart—even if it is a ghost? Other readers assumed I had some insight into how to contact the spirits of the dead. I don't. It's been my experience that they will float into my sphere of existence at their own will and whim. Try as I may, desire as I do, I can't for the life of me reach out and touch the dead. That's an advantage they hold over me.

Some folks wanted only to understand why the dead seem to sometimes hang around, and how to live a life of peaceful coexistence with them. In those cases I could offer only my beliefs and my assumptions—garnered from personal experiences as well as insight I gleaned while visiting haunted places and interviewing "hauntees." On a religious note, I believe in life after death. That being the case, it's no real surprise to me when a couple of my deceased relatives decide to show up from time to time. I try to tell folks that perhaps it's an honor to live with a spirit, as they may be trying to reach out to you for help or comfort. Ghosts should offer us a sense of peace in how they assure us that our physical existence does not come to a screeching halt after we've been pronounced dead.

I've had a great many people write me to express their satisfaction with my finished manuscript. Many said my first book was "entertaining" or "thought provoking." Some even complimented my writing style, calling it "relaxed" or "refreshing." On the other hand, I also had my critics, and they were perfectly willing to express their comments in the form of book reviews. One such critic said he liked the book well enough, but that I had no business referring to myself as a "professional ghosthunter" since I didn't take so much as a camera with me on my "investigations."

What I have to say next regarding that claim will most likely raise the ire of a good many people. *Just what the heck is a professional ghosthunter anyway?* All the fancy equipment in the world—infrared cameras, meters to measure temperature and electromagnetic fields and variations in the atmosphere, and whatever other devices professional ghosthunters may embrace in an effort to spook out a spook—has not proven the existence of ghosts at all. No amount of scientific efforts have been able to conclude that ghosts live among us.

Even those folks with professional training in the field of parapsychology have not produced the evidence necessary to prove that ghosts are real. The best they have is theory and palaver.

I admit I have had a great deal of so-called "evidence" thrust in front of my face to prove ghosts coexist with us. Little of it has bordered on being convincing. I've viewed dozens of photos containing what ghost afficionados refer to as "orbs"—balls of light that show up on their exposed film. When asked to explain this phenomenon, I agree with them that they obviously have balls of light in their photos. My question is, *How do you make the cognitive connection between those balls of light and a ghost?* Just because we cannot explain something, doesn't necessarily mean we have the right to explain it. The same holds true with photographs showing hazy white clouds cutting across the subject of the camera's lens. Sure, I can see those white clouds invading your picture, but how does that qualify as proof of ghostly presences? In short, for all their efforts, no "professional" ghosthunter has proven the existence of ghosts.

Why, then, do I believe in ghosts if their existence cannot be proven scientifically? It's simple. I don't need scientific proof. I have had numerous personal, subjective experiences with ghosts, often in the presence of other witnesses. The key word here is "subjective." I do not believe ghosts can be proven to exist through the means of objective measurements. As with all things spiritual, it is the subjective experience that breathes life into what we believe, every bit as much as empirical evidence defines the nature of the organic world around us. Sure, I have a few snapshots of ghosts, and I believe they really are ghosts. But that belief is based upon my personal, subjective experience at the time I snapped the shutter, not upon the actual photograph alone. There is no rational explanation for ghosts, because the experience of the paranormal is irrational—it makes no sense under controlled, scientific conditions, but all the sense in the world when experienced subjectively.

Perhaps this is why a ghost story is just a ghost story except to those who have had personal encounters with a specter or two. Maybe that's why so many people felt a kinship with my book, because it tries to express what they have already encountered for themselves.

In conclusion, I remain fascinated with what I call the reality of ghosts as a part of human existence. I intend to continue my "amateur and unscientific" exploration into this spooky realm for the rest of my remaining years. Who knows? Perhaps I'll decide to show up after my demise to terrorize and mystify a relative or two. And maybe someone will try to prove my existence when I do.

The Haunt Meter

BACK BY POPULAR demand is what I have affectionately dubbed the "Haunt Meter," a system which rates each haunted place according to the level of its scare quotient and frequency of paranormal activity.

The Haunt Meter simply uses the familiar system of ranking by stars. The higher the frights, the higher the number of stars. Since many of the stories I investigated turned out to be pure hokum, rating a mere one or two stars, they died an early death, falling victim to the dreaded "delete" key on my computer. I've included only those chapters that I believe to be both genuine, and genuinely frightening.

So, here it is again, Rev. Gerry's official Haunt Meter!

A pretty lame haunting,
not worthy of my efforts or your time.

The ghosts are there, but the scares aren't.

A good haunting—some chills and goose bumps.

Don't enter these places alone!
Eerie and lots of activity.

Watch your backside!
Macabre and downright frightening.

More
Haunted Michigan

Blanche

On reverse page: *A drawing of Blanche, a spirit often seen looking out the upstairs windows of the Jackson Antique Mall. See Chapter 7, "Antique Ghosts."* (by psychic Suki Wheeler)

Now This Is
Invasion of Privacy

Location of Haunting: A two-story, contemporary home with several acres of land on Oakwood Drive in Byron, Michigan.

Period of Haunting: The haunting began gently but insidiously about four years ago. In June of 2001, it suddenly and inexplicably intensified, running the gamut of paranormal activity. As of this writing, the overt actions of the spirits indicate they insist upon both terrorizing and fascinating the entire household.

Date of Investigation: I first heard about the rude behavior of these ghosts through a desperately worded e-mail sent to me via my publisher. The author of that e-mail was one Flo Cutcher, assuring me she was at her wits' end. Her frantic message prompted me to telephone her from my hotel room in Lincoln, Nebraska. That conversation could be likened to the gushing of a broken water main, with Flo literally pouring forth story after story of what the spirits were subjecting her to, and going on to say she had the overwhelming urge to just pack up and move out. A while after I returned home to Michigan, I made arrangements to visit her haunted abode, sometime in the middle of April, 2002.

Description of Location: Byron, Michigan, is a hamlet of about 500 people, northwest of Howell. The house in question is on a pastoral stretch of land. The Cutcher home is one of several along Oakwood Drive, each appearing to have a few acres of land attached to them. A pleasant, two-story home, it looks peaceful and serene, right down to the ducks and chickens traversing the yard. The owners are not desirous of ghost afficionados invading their privacy. The Western Michigan Ghost Hunters Society is presently involved in a full investigation of the ghostly activity therein, and photographs of their work at this address can be seen on their Web site (www.geocities.com/wmghost). One way to arrive at the domicile is to travel north on US-23 from Ann Arbor, exiting at M-59. Head west to Argentine Road and turn right. Proceed to Silver Lake Road and turn left. Go west to Dunhill Road and turn right. Follow that road north to Oakwood and turn right. The home in question is a short drive further.

The Haunt Meter: * * * * *

This appears to be one doozy of a haunted house, with many fascinating ingredients mixed into its ethereal pie. The activity here can be approached from many directions and viewpoints—paranormal, spiritual, and psychological. This haunting seems to cause investigators to ask more questions than they can possibly attempt to answer, which is one of the reasons I enjoyed my visit there so much.

Although she may not readily admit to it, it appears to me, as well as many others, that Flo is predisposed to experience otherworldly phenomena and has been since her rather interesting youth. When Flo was about nine years old, her parents rented a home in Fenton, Michigan, which, as any Michigan ghosthunter can tell you, is probably one of the most haunted cities in the state. The address she gives for that home is 11318 Hartland Road. At any rate, her parents moved their large family into that rambling old farmhouse, and oddities of a spectral sort seemed to permeate the place. Flo's mother, Mary, recalls one of the first of several strange encounters. "I was lying down in my bedroom, a room with windows on two sides," recalls Mary.

It was situated near the front of the house where every time a car would pass by the lights of the car would shine in one of the windows, depending upon which way the car was coming. Well, I was by myself and it was dark out. All of a sudden I saw a glowing light and there in front of me was a woman, just standing there looking at me. I could tell right away it wasn't someone alive, but I swear she was looking straight at me like she was wondering what I was doing there.

Mary kept the incident to herself, not wanting to frighten the children. She did share the encounter with her husband, who indicated he didn't believe in such poppycock as ghosts. The next day or so, he went to enroll the kids in their new school, and when he gave the address to the lady in the school office, she said she knew the house well, and that her grandmother had died in the house and was sometimes seen by guests and family. If that wasn't enough to raise his eyebrows a bit concerning the reality of ghosts, what followed proved to be the chaser.

Flo recalls that she and her three sisters shared a bedroom upstairs in the creepy old manse. "We had bunk beds to accommodate us all," she says,

and night after night my sisters and I would hear footsteps coming up the stairs. At first we thought it was Mom or Dad, and sometimes it would be. But mostly it wasn't them at all; it was a dark form, all hunched over. It would stop at the top step and stare into the room, watching us for a long time before just vanishing. We'd tell Dad about it, but he wouldn't believe us and said we girls just had wild imaginations.

Sometimes the girls would hear their names being called out—and would head downstairs to see what their parents wanted, only to be sent back to bed with the usual parental admonishment to stay put. "At that point," remembers Flo, "Mom and Dad were still swaying on the edge of belief and disbelief."

Flo and family lived in the house until she was about fourteen years old. Eerie flights of fancy escalated into outright horrific encounters. "We would always see that hunched-over figure of someone coming up the stairs," says Flo,

> but pretty soon he actually started coming into our rooms. Then one night he really scared the daylights out of me. I was in bed on the top bunk when out of the corner of my eye I could see him coming up the stairs again, all black and solid and hunched over. This time he seemed to scoot through the doorway and into the room, staying in the hunched-over position we always saw him in. Then he looked right up at me and I swear I shivered all over. It was the first time I had ever seen its face. He had a perfectly round, brilliantly white face with deep set black eyes. For a minute or so we just stared at each other and I couldn't move. Then, still hunched over, he started to scoot over to where my sisters were sleeping in their beds. One by one he would scoot over next to them, look at them for a minute and then look over and up at me, like he was making sure I was still watching. By now I'm sitting up in bed staring at him as he went from sister to sister. He kept this up, going from one sister to another, each time stopping to look up at me. Then, all of a sudden, he just appeared up on the foot of my bed. He sat there staring at me, and all I could see was this white, hideous face. In an instant he was gone and back on the floor again, all hunched over and perched next to one of my sister's beds. He would look first at her and then at me, back and forth, and then he leaned over my sister and just started to rise up off the floor, spreading his arms out and getting really huge. That's when I screamed and he just started to disappear.

The family didn't stay in that house much longer, as mother Mary soon joined her children in the conviction that harmful entities were running rampant throughout the place. "I finally had enough," says Mary, and told my husband there was no way I was staying there any longer. Besides, I had heard stories from people around Fenton that several people had been murdered at that place, mostly out by the old meat-packing shed. Maybe people were making some of that stuff up, but it was enough for me. We left!

I've related this story to you in the conviction that Flo seems to have a natural tendency to bump up against things that go bump in the night. Although the rest of her adolescent years were relatively ghost-free, it all started up again after she married her husband Ted.

> We had been married for a while, and decided we wanted to move to Howell. One evening our real estate agent took us to an old Victorian home we were interested in buying. We got to the house and the people living in it let us have the run of the place. Ted stayed downstairs to talk to the owners while the agent and I went upstairs. Just as we were about to go into one of the upstairs rooms, something grabbed me by the shoulders and slammed my head against the doorway. The real estate agent just jumped back all wide-eyed and then we both took off downstairs. A few moments later I told Ted I wasn't feeling well, and that it was time to leave. The agent never called to ask if we were interested in the place, and it's just as well, because there was no way I was going to buy a house like that.

For a bit, things seemed to settle down for Flo. She and Ted found a place in Howell they were comfortable with, and they spent a few years there—uninterrupted by devilish pranks—eventually selling the place and moving to the Byron area about four years ago. That is, of course, when she once again discovered she had encountered a house harboring a few added attractions.

From the outset, the family began to encounter eerie incidents. Flo tells of hearing heavy footsteps across the upstairs floor. "From the sound of it," says she,

> it had to have been a pretty heavy man, because that

area's carpeted and the clumping of the footsteps was really loud. This would happen at different times during the day or night, but usually when I was alone or the only one in the area, although my daughter has heard it, too.

Daughter Stefanie, now eighteen, has her own story to spin. "There were times when I was lying in bed, and all of a sudden I would feel someone get into bed with me—not sit on the bed—actually get into it with me," she says. "When I'd reach over to where it felt like the person must be, that part of the bed would be ice cold."

Another time, Stefanie had just gone to bed when a woman dressed in clothing from the 1880s nonchalantly floated past her. "I was just lying there reading a book and there she was. She had this really bright yellowish glow to her." Stefanie has since moved out on her own, but paranormal activity, she says, has followed her to her new house.

Although all family members have encountered activity of a weird sort, Ted has been mostly kept out of the ghostly loop. "Ted really didn't want to believe any of the stuff I was telling him," says Flo.

> He used to tease me about cracking up. But he has had a couple of small things happen to him that he admits are odd. Like one time he was upstairs on the computer, and he thought he could see black forms scooting past him out of the corner of his eye. And once, while he was sleeping in, I was on the landing outside our bedroom working on the computer when there was this tremendous boom on the floor. Ted flew out of the bedroom from a dead sleep and we searched the house but nothing was out of order that we could see.

Ted works an afternoon shift at one of the Big Three automotive plants, and Flo usually stays up late reading or watching television in her room until he returns home or she falls asleep. Sometimes son Brett, age twelve, lays on a pillow in his mother's room and they

The Cutcher bedroom, where ghosts are seen nightly.

watch a movie together. "One time," says Flo,

> I was in bed and Brett was lying on the floor. We were
> watching a rental and it was about eleven o'clock. I
> looked up to see a dark form walk into the room and
> move past the foot of my bed, between me and the
> fireplace. Then it moved on over toward Brett. It went
> between him and the television, and then past him and
> over to the nightstand on my side of the bed. It stood
> there a few seconds, and then it was gone.

These dark forms seem to be the essence of Flo and
Ted's excellent adventure. Flo encounters them regularly. "Every night these dark forms would either come
in through the bedroom door or pass from the master
bath hallway into the bedroom," she says.

> They always seemed to walk over toward the far side of
> the bedroom where my nightstand is, and then disap-
> pear. Eventually I got to where I really didn't want to
> see them anymore so I started to leave the bathroom
> light on. The brightness of the light keeps me from

seeing them so much.

The master bath has a story all its own. It is a gorgeous room including a large garden tub with jets to soothe the aching muscles, a separate shower, linen closet, and all the other facilities one needs to meet one's needs and refreshen one's demeanor. As inviting as the whirlpool tub appears, Flo admits to having used it only two or three times since moving into the house. "I can't bring myself to use that tub," says Flo, "it just creeps me out."

Flo apparently has good reason to be creeped out by the whirlpool. At both ends of the tub Flo has hung

The master bath. One male ghost hides behind the plant and watches the women. He was supposedly hiding there when this photo was taken.

beautiful vines. They have grown to such lengths that their extremities line the inside rim of the tub until they meet one another. It is behind one of these hanging plants that a man stands and watches her whenever she's in the bathroom. "This guy," says Flo,

> stays behind the plant on the edge of the tub and stares at me. I can only see him from about the waist up, and he's not solid at all. He sort of shimmers. I sense him there almost all the time, and when I stop and look I can see him shimmering behind the plant. There's no real color to him at all, he's sort of like that creature in the *Predator* movie. He's tough to see until he moves, and then you can see the outline of him.

While I was visiting Flo's place, I couldn't resist taking the obligatory nickel tour. I was struck by the beauty of the house, and if the master bath is as inviting to the ghost as it is to me, then I don't blame him for hanging out in there. When Flo showed me that area, I asked her if the guy was there behind the plant. She stood still for a moment, staring at the plant, and finally said he was. I must admit I couldn't see anything but vines and leaves, but Flo was insistent. I snapped several pictures in hopes of catching his image, but to no avail. Flo maintains he stood there the whole time we were in the bathroom, just watching us. "Every time I take a shower, he's there. I can see him as I'm getting ready to shower, but there's a wall dividing the shower from the bath tub, so I don't have his peeping eyes watching me," she says. "But one time, just recently, I was showering and when I looked through the glass door I could see a man standing by the linen closet watching me. When I slid open the shower door, he was gone."

As our tour continued, I followed Flo and Stefanie down into the basement, which has been sectioned off into three rooms. The stairway opens up into one large room the family uses as—what else—a family room. It boasts the requisite family decor, a large television set, pool table, couch, and chairs. To the right of the stair-case is another room, this one housing the furnace and utility accesses. To the left of the stairway is a room that once served as Stefanie's bedroom, but is now in use as a craft and sewing room for Flo.

I listened in rapt attention as Flo and Stefanie recounted some of their experiences down in the bowels of the home. "There are a lot of times," says Flo,

> when I come down here to work on my sewing—I make doll clothing—and I'll see the image of a woman from another time standing over by the doorway of the furnace room. She seems pleasant enough, and I'm not really frightened by her. She seems to be from around

The utility room doorway, where a female ghost, apparently from the early 1900s, peers out at the Cutcher family.

the turn-of-the-century, with the long puffy blouse and the long skirt down to her ankles. She's actually quite attractive. As soon as she's aware of me looking at her, she sort of scoots back into the darkened furnace room, and then usually disappears. Sometimes, however, she'll sort of hide behind the furnace and peek around it to watch what I'm doing.

I asked Flo is she ever thought of trying to communicate with this lady, and she said she had.

There's been several times when I would speak to her as she stood there looking at me. I'd ask things like who she was or what she wanted, but she would just slip real fast into the furnace room. Other times, I'd actually go in there and try to find her, but she would disappear.

This chic lady from another age is apparently not the only ghost haunting the downstairs area. Both Stefanie and Flo maintain there is a shadowy form that emerges from the back corner of the family room, and then moves silently along the paneled wall toward the stairway. "It's pretty much the same every time I see it," says Stefanie,

you'll be watching TV, and all of a sudden he is just there, off in the corner. It has form, but it's more like a thick shadow. When you look at him, he speeds up, and when he gets to the end of the wall, he's just gone. I don't get a real good feeling from that one.

As Stefanie spoke those tentative words, Flo was nodding her head in assent. "The black form is really creepy. I don't like being around when he's here. It just feels strange."

As I jotted down notes, I was seated in a chair with my back to the far wall. I was facing both the entrance to the stairway and the couch in front of me, where Flo and Stefanie sat. At one point, there was a moment of silence as they awaited the completion of my note-taking, but that silence was suddenly punctuated by

Flo.

"Did you see that, Stef?"

"Yes," Stefanie said, "I did."

When I asked if I could be let in on the festivities, Flo said, "Just now I saw that black form float out of the wall, and then scoot down toward the furnace room. We both saw it."

I was struck by how nonchalantly they referred to this uninvited arrival, sort of like it happens every day, which it just may. I immediately looked around behind me, but as is often my luck, I was too slow on the draw. It mattered little, according to Flo, because by the time they mentioned it, he was already gone, slipped off into the furnace room and out of sight.

Tired of having to endure the ramblings of their spirits, sick of the thoughtless intrusions into their privacy, Flo made contact with a consortium of folks who investigate hauntings around the state. Arrangements were made for a visit, and when they arrived they had lugged along with them all the equipment one would expect a ghosthunter to possess.

"They were really nice people," says Flo.

There were four of them, and they came in the afternoon. They asked a lot of questions about what we had been experiencing and what areas of the house were the most active. Then they set up their equipment and started checking things out right away. What's interesting is that one of the men, a guy who says he's not even particularly gifted psychically, got really excited right off the bat, saying he could sense the spirits all around the house, and even see some of them. He would run over to a corner of a room and stretch out his hands saying, "He's right here, standing next to me," and when photos were taken of that area, they came out with balls of lights in them that no one else had seen.

The ghosthunters excitedly researched the house,

perusing every inch, upstairs and down. They spent the night down in the basement, videotaping and snapping pictures, and also employing their meters and tape recorders. In the morning the ever hospitable Flo served everyone bacon and eggs, and the conversation was geared, naturally, around the experiences of the night. In short, they were thrilled with how active the house had been, and showed Flo several photographs with "anomalies" in them. As they exited, exhausted but pumped up by their results, they promised to return, and to bring with them a woman who is reported to be quite gifted in a psychic sense of the word. As of the date of this writing, that had yet to occur.

As my visit neared its end, we sat around the kitchen table, where coffee and cookies were graciously presented me. I brought up the subject that I had seen a good many antiques scattered throughout the house, and Flo indicated that antiques were something she just couldn't do without. I asked her if things were quieter before she had accumulated so many ancient pieces, and she said she really couldn't say. I wondered aloud if perhaps some of those antiques entered her house with some strings attached, namely a previous deceased owner or two. I have heard that sometimes people get quite taken with their possessions and, upon death, refuse to let go. It's interesting to note that the fireplace in the master bedroom sports antique photographs of people Flo doesn't know. Could that have something to do with how heavily that area of the house is haunted?

I thanked Flo and her family for allowing me the opportunity to spend the evening with them and apologized for having stolen so much of it away from them. She wanted to send me on my way with some homemade cookies, but I declined, having decided months earlier that my paunch was protruding sufficiently already. I did ask if I could snap a photo or two on the way out, and permission was given.

The setting sun had not yet fully disappeared into the horizon, so I had enough light to take a few outdoor photos. I snapped a shot of the shed, where Flo keeps her chickens and ducks, and where she and other family members have often seen the image of a man dressed in casual clothing and wearing a ball cap standing and looking around the place like it was his. Then I shot a few photos of the exterior of the house, hoping to catch an anomaly of my own peeping out through one of the upstairs windows. I guess I'm not as lucky as the ghosthunters, as my photos showed only a shed full of chickens and a nice home in the country. Such is my fate on these outings.

Author's note: This story gave me fits when I tried to put it all down on computer diskette. I typed half of the manuscript, then saved it on disk, and backed it up as I always do onto two other disks. I do this with all my stories, and even keep the disks separated from one another in different rooms. It's just a precaution I take to protect my work. I called up the story on disk, and completed it. Then I backed the whole thing up once again on two other disks. When I called the story up to print it out a couple months later, the last third of the story—several pages—were missing. One at a time I slid the other two disks into my computer, and they too were missing the same sections of the story. I know there was no mistake on my part, because before I had filed the disks away, I had checked each of them individually to make certain the story was intact, which again is something I do with every tale I pen. Under a deadline to get my completed manuscript to the publisher in Chicago, I was understandably livid that one of my best stories was suddenly and inexplicably incomplete. This is not the first time I've experienced unexplained lapses such as this, and I expressed my anger rather inappropriately for someone of my social position and particular profession. But since I was alone in the house at the time, the only one ashamed of me is me. I am full of wonder as to the possibility that one of the spirits of the house in Byron was playing games with me. If so, someone certainly needs to play games with them. Paybacks are nasty.

2

The Ghost of the Grieving Gentleman

Location of Haunting: Northview Cemetery in Dearborn, Michigan. The cemetery is located at the intersection of Cherry Hill and Outer Drive.

Period of Haunting: This haunting is quite recent, and judging by the nature of it, there is no reason to believe it does not continue. Ghosts looking for a long-lost loved one seem to be cursed to carry on their tragically romantic pining throughout the decades.

Date of Investigation: Spring of 2002.

Description of Location: Dearborn, Michigan, is an upscale community whose border is shared with Detroit on the east and Inkster on the west. For most of his life, this city was home to Henry Ford, whose name is synonymous with the automobile. The world headquarters for The Ford Motor Company is still in Dearborn, on Michigan Avenue. The Henry Ford Estate, Fairlane, is situated there, as is the Henry Ford Museum and Greenfield Village, a massive expanse of land offering historical exhibits of great importance. Greenfield Village offers glimpses of life during the early days of Michigan, as well as exhibits of Thomas Edison's laboratory and the Wright Brothers' home. The Henry Ford Museum has, as one would expect, one of the finest displays of antique automobiles to be found anywhere. It also harbors such curiosities as the glass vial purported to contain the last breath exhaled by inventor

Thomas Edison, who was admired to no end by Mr. Ford.

While roaming the area in search of paranormal oddities to feed your imagination, don't forget to feed the body as well. Allow me to suggest Buddy's Pizza on Michigan Avenue right downtown. It has been consistently voted the best pizza in the state by all major television stations and newspapers. Maybe it's because they know enough to put the pepperoni under the cheese before baking. Anyway, Buddy's alone is worth the trip.

The Haunt Meter: * *
Remember, the haunt meter determines the scare quotient, and even though two stars means it isn't frightening, it's still a good tale.

Northview Cemetery is attractive as cemeteries go. Well-manicured lawns cover a sweeping acreage. Across from one of its borders is a city park. It is from this vantage point that the gentleman ghost was first encountered.

Allison Ridge (real name withheld for reasons soon apparent) was going through a rather distasteful divorce. As luck would have it, so was her new boyfriend. At times such as this, it's practically imperative to have someone to confide in, and, naturally, they chose one another.

"Things weren't exactly going very well for me," says Allison.

> Martin and I weren't comfortable meeting out in the open yet, so we had to find places to meet that were sort of out of the way. On this particular night, we agreed to meet at the park next to the cemetery around eleven.

It was a pleasant enough October night, a bit on the chilly side, when Allison pedaled her bicycle down the

sidewalks and into the park to meet her beau. Martin
had arrived before her, and had staked out a picnic
table for them. "We sat and talked till well after midnight," says Allison.

We had a lot in common and really enjoyed one
another's company. We just made small talk like people in love do and were sort of absorbed with one
another. I remember the night was clear and the moon
was almost full. We had been talking for a while when
all of a sudden I saw this man out in the cemetery, just
standing there. He was kind of tall, and he was
wearing a long, dark coat that was billowing out in the
wind. I sort of pick up on strange stuff, so I knew right
away this guy wasn't real, that he was a spirit of some
sort. I asked Martin if he could see the guy, and he
said he couldn't see anything. That didn't matter to
me, I just felt compelled to jog on over and see what
was up. The man was standing on a small hill, right
next to a tall monument and some big pine trees. I just
had to see if he was real or what. I stopped at the fence
and sort of said with my mind, "who are you?" Immediately, the name "Edgar Lininger" just shot into my
head. I stood there looking at him for several minutes,
and he appeared to be from sometime around the
1920s or '30s by the way he was dressed. He looked
like he was in his late twenties, but old enough to be
someone of wealth and stature. When I asked him
what he wanted, he said he was "looking for Annie,"
and his voice had an accent to it, I think it was
German. Then he just started to fade away. He sort of
dissolved into dots and was gone. I'll never forget what
he looked like—he was impeccably dressed, a really
good-looking guy.

Although Martin claimed he hadn't seen anything
other than Allison standing at the fence, she was struck
enough by the encounter to feel compelled to check the
matter out. She perused the cemetery records, looking
for someone with the name Edgar Lininger, but to no
avail. She made her way on over to the county seat to
search the death certificates, but again ended up

empty-handed. She decided to check out the cemetery's headstones for herself.

"I thought I'd start with the cemetery where I'd seen Edgar," says Allison.

> I thought maybe the death records had been lost or misplaced, and that maybe I'd just find his tombstone on my own. Again, though, I didn't have any luck at all. Then, sort of as a last resort, I went to the historical society for help. I didn't know if I should tell them why I wanted to find Edgar, so I kept the events of the night I met him to myself. I couldn't believe it, but they actually had a record of him. It seems he was from Germany originally and had made a bit of a name for himself as a local businessman. He had never married, so there was really no family to track. That's when I figured that maybe Annie had been the love of his life, and for some reason he had lost her. And if he was looking for her in a cemetery, well, maybe she had died before he did.

Allison went to the cemetery in question and actually found Edgar's tombstone. It indicated he had passed on in 1927, not yet thirty years of age. While paying homage there, she realized that she felt an emotional connection to Edgar and decided to plant a few flowers around his grave. "Actually," says Allison,

> I felt really sorry for him. I mean, he was looking for his lost love. Maybe that's why he showed himself to me, because I had just ended a relationship of my own and had just recently found a new love. Maybe the strength of that new love drew him to me.

Allison drove over to a local greenhouse and picked up some small plants she thought to be appropriate for Edgar's grave site. She planted them around the headstone and watered them from a gallon jug she had brought along with her. "I didn't have enough water," she says,

> and I started looking around for a place to fill the jug up, but I couldn't see any spigots anywhere. Then this

lovely old woman came up from behind me and offered to let me use what was left in her watering can. I finished watering the plants and thanked her. Then I looked to see if everything around the grave was suitable. I had just looked away from the woman for a second or two, but when I turned around to thank her again, she was gone.

From Allison's position she could scan the length of the cemetery, but she couldn't find a trace of that lovely old woman. "There's no way in the world she could have gotten out of sight that fast," she says.

She was just gone in an instant, watering can and all. I must have wandered around the rest of the cemetery for an hour looking for signs of her, but she wasn't there. Then a really spooky thought occurred to me— what if that old woman was Annie, and she was grateful for my decorating the grave of her loved one, Edgar? What if he had died before her and she had lived to a ripe old age, always missing him. Maybe now they were separated in death by being in different cemeteries. After all, Edgar's plot is by itself, and no one named Annie is anywhere nearby.

3

No Help with the Wicked

Location of Haunting: A two-story, wood and brick dwelling in a relatively quiet subdivision of Dearborn Heights. Although the exact address is not given, its backyard borders one of the larger cemeteries in Dearborn/Dearborn Heights. While the residents were leaning toward allowing me to give the exact address, it was my decision to obscure it, as the nature of this haunting would most likely draw great attention to the family. As the haunting they are dealing with is frightening in the extreme, the added stress of strangers staring at them from their front lawn would be most unkind, and I genuinely like this dear family.

Period of Haunting: The home was built by the current owners in 1970, and they are the only family to have lived there. These good people have been terrorized by their haunting, which has escalated markedly throughout the years, commencing not long after they moved in. While there are times when the frightening experiences settle down a bit, hardly a week passes without several days of intense phenomena.

Date of Investigation: I spent a great deal of time in the home with the family in the summer of 2001. Follow-up consisted of repeated phone calls and e-mails. The investigation continued through the early summer of 2002, with more to follow.

Description of Location: I admit I have struggled

greatly with whether or not to put into print the actual and exact location of this dwelling. I will say this much—the home is over thirty years old and quite charming. By all appearances, it is simply one of many "normal" homes tucked peacefully away within a normal subdivision. It has a well-manicured lawn, a swimming pool in the backyard, and a few cherry trees. It is located near Telegraph and Ford Roads, and the huge area behind it had once been a driving range. That area is now a cemetery. The best I can do for you is to direct you to take US-12 (Michigan Avenue) west from Detroit, turning north onto Telegraph. When you get to Ford Road, turn right once again. You'll see a cemetery on the north side of Ford Road. At this point you are practically there. *Please exercise civility and respect, and do not invade this family's privacy, as they deserve to be left alone.*

Description of Family: This family, whom I shall refer to as the Kennedys, are what you would call good Irish-Catholics, and not simply in name only. They are quite proud of their Irish ancestry and have traced it back to the Emerald Isle. As for the expression of their Christian faith, mass is something they simply refuse to miss. They faithfully observe the religious holidays and take seriously their roles in the Church.

The family consists of six persons—father Devon, mother Cybil, and daughters Stacey, Kerry, Mary, and Kaitlynn. The lone man of the house is in his seventies and retired. Cybil is employed in the Wayne County Court system. Stacey, Mary, and Kerry are in their thirties and have moved into homes of their own nearby. The youngest daughter, Kaitlynn, attends graduate school in California, but still maintains her legal residence with her parents, spending summers and vacation periods back in Michigan. All are professional persons, well educated, and quite respected in their fields. The home is meticulously maintained, adorned with the important symbols of their faith.

Author's Note: I have been interested in hauntings since I was a child. I have experienced strange doings in a plethora of places. I have seen firsthand the spirits of the dead. I have spent many a night alone in haunted dwellings. I have videotaped ghosts. I have audiotaped ghosts. I have taken photographs of ghosts. I have heard their voices as they have spoken to me and, on occasion, I have even had a couple of them violate my personal space. After a lifetime of fascination with ghosts and about fifteen years of actively seeking them out, I must admit I have never met a family as terrified of the spirits within their home as this family. I don't believe I have ever encountered a home this incredibly active.

The Haunt Meter: * * * * *
It doesn't get any worse than this, folks.

I was first contacted by Kaitlynn. She had read my book and asked if I could make contact with her, as she and her family had been for years tormented by what they thought to be a bevy of negative spirits.

Kaitlynn is a charming, intelligent young woman. Her demeanor is calm, and she chooses her words carefully. Although the entire family (with one interesting exception) has been terrorized by the several entities within their home, it is Kaitlynn who has been singled out as the main recipient of horrific encounters.

Kaitlynn informed me that the strange events began to escalate over twenty years ago, when her sisters were teenagers. Sister Kerry had retired to her bedroom for the night and was lying there daydreaming (is there a word for daydreaming at night?). At any rate, she looked up toward the ceiling of her bedroom and was stunned to see, over in one corner above her, the shadow of a cloaked man hovering a few feet off the floor. He appeared to have a dark hood covering his head, and where the face should have been, there was an ominous, ebony void. As she fixed her gaze upon him, he very fluidly floated from one corner of the room to the next, eventually exiting through the doorway and down the hall to her sister Stacey's room.

"I really didn't want to believe what I was seeing," says Kerry.

Practically all my life up till then we had all had weird things happen around us, but nothing like this. I watched this thing scoot down the hall and into my sister's room. As terrible as it sounds, I was glad it left my room no matter where it went. I was pretty shook up about it, but didn't do anything at all—I was really too scared to do anything. Then, a few days later, I asked Stacey if she noticed anything strange going on in her room lately, and she said she had, that a couple nights earlier she had seen a black-hooded entity float down the hallway and into her room, where it stayed for a minute or two and then seemed to evaporate into the ceiling. When I heard that, I was really scared.

Although the two older sisters were teenagers before they experienced such overt spectral activity, Kaitlynn has dealt with the spirits of the house as far back as she can recall. "I remember when I was quite young," says Kaitlynn,

and I would play outside in the backyard on my swingset, all by myself. As the swing would go forward toward the house, I'd see a face in the upstairs bedroom window looking out at me. This would happen time after time, and it really scared me. I could never make out the fine details of it, and I couldn't tell if it was a man or a woman, but it would always stare at me, and I could tell even then that it didn't like me. It always appeared in Stacey's bedroom window, and only when I was alone. It got to the point where, if I played in the backyard, I'd try real hard not to look at that window, and if I ever did, it was almost always there, watching me. I just got the sense it was dark and ugly.

No child ought to experience the macabre firsthand.

For Kaitlynn, it was an integral part of growing up. "Not long after I started seeing the face in the bedroom window," she says,

> other things started happening to me. Things I was way too young to even begin to understand. I started seeing the figures of different people walking in the hallway upstairs. I'd be in my bedroom, and they'd pass by the doorway. I'd look out into the hallway, and sometimes I'd see them going into another bedroom, or into the bathroom, or even down the stairway.

As if this blatant disrespect for one's privacy wasn't enough, the spirits within those walls began to speak to Kaitlynn. "Once," says Kaitlynn,

> I was upstairs and walked past an empty bedroom. As I passed the doorway, I saw an old woman lying on the bed in there. I stopped to look at her, and she called me by name and told me to come into the room. There was no way I was going to do that, and I just turned around and went downstairs. It reached a point where when I went upstairs, I could almost tell if she was going to be in that room, lying on the bed.

As Kaitlynn grew into her teenaged years, the hauntings became more severe. Soon she was seeing spirits practically everywhere in the house, as were her older sisters. Whereas Stacey and Kerry saw them sporadically, Kaitlynn began encountering them regularly. "It seemed like there was no place I could go where I wouldn't encounter a ghost," she says.

> I remember one afternoon, sometime in late spring, I needed to go up to my room to get some things for a homework project I was working on. I always dreaded having to go up there by myself, but what are you going to do? I went upstairs and into my bedroom. I picked up the things I needed and stepped out into the hallway. As soon as I did, I saw this man standing between me and the stairway. I remember he was a tall man, not at all good-looking, and he was wearing a tie. He started walking toward me and was looking right at

me. I was so scared of him that I actually just reacted out of fear, and ran right through him and down the stairs. I remember a deep coldness as I passed through him. There was no way I was going to stay up there with him around.

It is interesting to note that not every family member has encountered the strange phenomena that permeates their household. Devon, father of the tormented girls, insists no ghosts were included in his closing costs. He will not admit to having seen anything unusual inside his home, but is reminded by his family of an unsettling experience or two he has had out in the backyard. "One time," says Kaitlynn,

> my father was outside in the backyard. It was late in the evening during the summer, and the pool was full. He was in the back of the yard, out by the cherry trees, and when he looked back toward the house, he saw a little boy standing near the pool. He said the little boy had dark pants on, but no shirt, and my father was afraid he might fall in the water and drown. As he walked toward him, the little boy seemed to just vanish. He tried to justify it by saying that maybe he had looked away for a moment and the little boy ran off real fast, except that excuse didn't work because another time my father was in the house, and when he looked out into the backyard, he saw the same strange boy standing out there again. He finally admitted it was a weird experience, but he still tries to dismiss all the things we say we encounter in the house.

A side note about that backyard concerns the aforementioned cherry trees. They spring up from the rear of the yard, near the fence, and have been known in the past to produce an abundance of luscious, sweet fruit. However, it appears the humans of the household need to be on their toes if they wish to partake of their flavorful delights. "There have been times," says Kaitlynn,

> when the cherries were ripe for picking, and the trees were full. We'd get up the next morning and look

outside only to discover no cherries on the trees at all. They'd be totally bare. Not only were the trees bare, but there wouldn't even be any cherries anywhere on the ground. It was like someone came in during the night and just stripped them all away. Now, there's no way that could happen, and even if you don't believe in ghosts or strange events, how do you explain this?

Good question.

I visited with the Kennedys for several hours one summer's evening and found them to be very congenial hosts. Mrs. Kennedy even insisted on running out to the drugstore to purchase some film for my camera, as I hadn't realized there was none in my camera bag when I left home. They seemed to be genuinely delighted to meet me and expressed their hope that I could explain to them why such strange and bizarre activity seemed to plague them.

As I always do while researching chapters for one of my books, I asked those family members present a battery of questions designed to determine what, if any, stress they have been under in recent months (aside from the haunting, of course); how their family relationships were progressing (steady as a rock); what sort of religious views and values they adhere to (strong, strict, practicing Catholics); and just what they thought was behind the discourteous behavior of their uninvited house guests (they had no idea). The basic results of my intrusive questioning (which they quite cheerfully went along with) was that this was a quite normal family caught up in quite abnormal circumstances. The haunting of their home spanned several decades and touched the lives of each family member, as well as the lives of many friends and relatives.

As can be the case with ghosts parading through your lives, it can be somewhat difficult to maintain private relationships. How, for instance, does one explain to a visiting boyfriend that when he comes to call he may be received by ghosts? Such was the case for

Kaitlynn in the spring of 1999, when a former boyfriend dropped by one evening. "We spent the evening together in the family room in the back of the house," says Kaitlynn.

> We had some snacks and visited with my parents, too. After they went to bed, we stayed downstairs to watch television. We were sitting on the couch watching a movie when, out of the corner of our eyes, we saw a figure crawling on all fours. We looked over and could see it crawling from one end of the living room to the other, where it finally went underneath a table and then disappeared into the living room wall. I was pretty scared, and so was he. I asked him to describe what he saw, and it was identical to what I had seen. It seems like it was a man, and that he was trying to sneak from one end of the living room to the other, but at the same time it felt like he wanted us to see him. My boyfriend went home a little while later, and he was still pretty shaken.

I announced I would like to take some photographs of the interior of the home. When I asked which rooms were most active, I was informed I could pretty much take my pick. Since the upstairs hallway and bedrooms were mentioned as a main locale for wandering souls, I suggested I begin there and asked Kaitlynn's sister Kerry if she would mind going up to her old bedroom so I could get a photo of her there. She told me she would be glad to do so, but that there was really no way she was going to go up there by herself. If I wanted to snap my shutter, she would wait until my camera was loaded so she would have some company up there. A moment later, she explained her reasoning.

"I can't tell you how many times I've been attacked in that room," said Kerry.

> It started a few years ago, when I was still living at home. I had gone to bed one night, and I just had this really eerie feeling. It's like you can almost tell sometimes when they are around. I hadn't been in bed long

when I felt something grab my feet and hold them. I sort of froze in terror, and I couldn't really move. Then this black, evil form rose up from the foot of my bed and slowly hovered over me. Then it floated down on top of me and pressed me down real hard on the mattress. I couldn't move a muscle, it was like it had taken full control of me physically. I couldn't even scream. I was so scared I started to think the words of the Lord's Prayer, and pretty soon I was able to speak. I kept saying the prayer out loud, and pretty soon it sort of lifted off me and disappeared. It was like it couldn't stand the prayer.

Such attacks by this malevolent entity became all-too-frequent an occurrence for Kerry and seemed to escalate in intensity. Eventually, when she was old enough, she moved out of the house. Though on her own now for quite some time, she is still very close to her family and returns often for visits. When she first started doing so, she would sometimes spend the night in her old bedroom, only to discover that the spirits of the house were still bent toward harassing her. Today, she still visits regularly, but rarely remains for the night. "I'm terrified to be up there alone," she says, "it's bad enough that whatever it is that's after me has even followed me to my apartment."

True enough, Kerry admits she feels as though at least one of the entities in her parents' home has taken up residence across town, or at least visits from time to time. Strange, inexplicable events haunt her on a regular basis. "I know it's whatever is in my folks' house," she says, "but I also know it can attach itself to you and go where you go. These things, whatever they are, are not bound to a particular place."

In 1994, Kaitlynn had just begun high school, where she was a baton twirler with the school band. "I was in the basement," says Kaitlynn,

practicing my baton routine. When I looked up, I saw my grandmother, who had died two years earlier, watching me. That's not the only time I've seen her, and I think maybe others have seen her here, too.

When Kaitlynn relates these interruptions of the ordinary, she speaks of them—even the most frightening of them—in a calm manner. It's almost as though they have become such a natural extension of her life's experiences that, even though from time to time she is very frightened, she has come to understand they are now a normal part of her existence. I have asked her about this attitude of calm expectance and have suggested that perhaps she is strongly tuned in to the activities of the spirit world. Kaitlynn assures me that she is indeed tuned in and that she also believes she must be some sort of magnet for the supernatural. Her strong faith, I believe, makes her somewhat reluctant to open up more fully, and that's to be respected.

When Kaitlynn was a senior in high school, she was employed part-time at the local Dairy Queen. Sometimes she would work until quite late in the evening, returning to a sleeping home. "Once in particular," she says,

> I came home pretty late after working all evening. I had put my laundry in the dryer before I had left for work, so I went down there to get it, to take it up to my room. When I got down there, the dryer was wide open, and all my laundry was strewn all over the basement floor, like someone had taken it and thrown it all over the place.

"About three weeks after the dryer episode," says Kaitlynn,

> I got home from the Dairy Queen about midnight. In our house you have to walk past the kitchen doorway to go upstairs to the bedrooms. Just as I walked past, I heard the door of the microwave open. I went in and closed it and, about the time I got to the foot of the stairway, I heard it open up again. It's the kind of microwave that has a handle you have to pull to open. I went back in, closed it, tugged on the handle to make

sure it was shut tightly, and left the room again. Then the kitchen light suddenly came on, and I heard the microwave door open again. I went in again, shut the door of the microwave and turned out the kitchen light. I went into the family room for a minute, then headed toward the stairs again. When I got there, the kitchen light was on again and the microwave door was pulled all the way open. What's worse, now the kitchen door that opens up into the garage was wide open.

What really puzzled Kaitlynn was that the home security system had been set to detect any intruders at the time of these disturbances. It is the sort of system that indicates with a buzzing noise if there are open doors or windows. "I checked to see if the alarm was set, and the red light was glowing which indicates that the alarm is armed," she says.

It's impossible for that door to be open with the alarm on and not have that buzzer going off. I could strongly sense the presence of a spirit in the kitchen with me, so I real quick-like started running up the stairs to my room. On the landing of the stairway there's a big mirror my mother had hung. As I passed the mirror, I could see the spirit in the mirror, following behind me.

The Kennedy family is unable to find any comfortable periods of repose, as these strange happenings never seem willing to offer them any rest. There appears to be no rhyme or reason to what takes place in their home, or who will show up to terrorize them. "Once," says Cybil,

I was straightening up around the house a bit, and I went into my bedroom upstairs to put some things away. When I looked out into the hallway, I saw a strange man walking past the bedrooms and toward the stairs. He was carrying a large, black bag. I have no idea who he was or what was in that bag, but it terrified me to see someone walking around upstairs who didn't belong there.

Cybil had a more intense encounter while bedded down for what she intended to be a good night's sleep. "Everything seemed fine that night," she says,

It was around Thanksgiving time, and Kaitlynn was home from college. Things had been busy with all the holiday preparations going on, but nothing was out of the ordinary. I went to bed and fell right to sleep. A couple of hours later, probably around 1 or 2 A.M., I felt a hand pushing my head down hard against the pillow. When I opened my eyes, it was my mother. It only lasted for a moment or so, and then she went away. I can't for the life of me understand why she would have done that to me, if she was trying to warn me about something, or what. It doesn't surprise me that it happened when Kaitlynn was home from school, because this sort of thing happens a great deal when she's home with us. It even happens to her while she's away at Albion.

Indeed, Kaitlynn's having moved into a house near her college didn't lessen the eerie experiences. It appears that wherever she goes, an entity or two follows. "I moved into a house at 110 N. Berrien Street with some friends," relates Kaitlynn.

It was a great location, really close to the college. Not long after I moved in, some of the things that were happening back home were happening there. In the middle of the night my bed would start shaking—you could actually see it moving. Sometimes, someone would grab my foot and squeeze it really hard. I quite often got the overwhelming sense that there was someone in the room with me, an entity of some sort, but I could never determine whether it was a man or a woman. It was like I was constantly being watched and whoever it was hated me. A couple of times, my roommates would talk about strange things in the house, too, and when I told them about my history with ghosts, they really got freaked out.

At the end of the Christmas break of 1998, Kaitlynn was upstairs in Kerry's former bedroom. She was packing her things to go back to Albion College. "The radio was playing softly," she says,

> and I was folding clothes to put into my bags. From inside the bedroom closet I heard three distinct knocks, like someone would do if they wanted to come into your room. I opened the closet door thinking maybe something had fallen over and made the knocking noises, but I really should have known better. When I opened the door, everything was fine in there; in fact, all that was in there were a couple of coats. There wasn't anything that could have fallen over. So, I dismissed what had happened, closed the door, and about ten minutes later the knocking started again, in a set of three. I went downstairs to get my parents because I was really scared. They came up and we all went through the room real well, but we couldn't determine what could have made the knocking noise.

(Author note: On more than one occasion, while writing chapters for my book, I've had strange things occur that I couldn't explain, such as missing manuscript sections or flashes of light interrupting my concentration. While reporting this incident of the knocking on the closet door, I was interrupted several times by what sounded like the rapping of knuckles on the window next to my computer desk. Each time I checked it out, but there was nothing in evidence to have caused such a disturbance. Nonetheless, it continued until this section of the chapter was completed.)

At the time of my visit, Kaitlynn was once again home from Albion. "I knew I was going to have to stay in that same bedroom again," she says,

> and I was psyching myself up to move back in there. I just know that whatever had been in that bedroom can read our minds. Well, I was closing my bedroom door and telling myself that nothing was in there, that I was all by myself, that nothing could get in, and that I couldn't see anybody if the door was closed. I turned off the light, put the bedside lamp on, and climbed into bed. Three minutes later I heard footsteps in the hall,

which is always a common occurrence, and then three knocks were made on my door. Both my parents were asleep at the time. I opened the door and called out for my mom, and when I stepped through the door and into the hallway, I stepped into freezing cold. That's about the time I decided I could no longer sleep alone in the house, that I had to think of something different. But I did stick it out a while longer.

By August of 1999, Kaitlynn says she had finally had enough terrorizing in that bedroom, and she began spending her nights tucked away in a sleeping bag on the floor of her parents' bedroom. That's when she says she experienced her most frightening incident. "I had gone to bed as usual," she says,

and after a while I had fallen asleep. I was awakened by a strong sense of someone being next to me. I opened my eyes and I could see feet next to my head. I looked up, and even though I couldn't make out a head, let alone a face, I really felt like I had made eye contact with him. I say "him" because I really felt it was the presence of a man. I closed my eyes, and pretended not to notice him. He then moved around to my feet and shoved me so hard that I physically moved forward and hit my head hard against the bedroom wall. Then all of a sudden it climbed on top of me and I experienced such a strong feeling of electricity going through me I thought I would suffocate. Then it rose up and scooted out of the room. I was so wired and scared that I couldn't sleep for two days.

This house is so very active that it's difficult to keep track of all the ghosts and evil entities wafting from room to room. There are men and women of varying ages, dark forms that scoot across the ceilings and floors, little boys in the backyard, at least one grandparent trying desperately to get their attention, and who knows how many unidentifiable spirits moving around the hallways at will. Such a fullness of activity and high number of entities leads one to naturally ask, *Why this house?* and *Why this family? Is there someone or some-*

thing that draws them?

What's interesting about the nature of this haunting, is that so much of the activity has increased in intensity within the past five or six years. Of particular note here is that in 1996 the family felt they had put up with enough nonsense and sleepless nights and decided to call upon their family priest for help. Enter one Father Stanley Creger (name changed), who was, in Kaitlynn's terms, "very skeptical" about what he had been told about the house. He agreed to come over and went through the home, offering the promised blessing. Kaitlynn tells me the visit was for the purpose of exorcising whatever was within their walls, and that at first things went relatively well. However, when the good Father entered her parents' bedroom, the figure of Christ fell off the crucifix that hangs on their wall. Then, as he ventured down into the basement and began saying his prayers, he felt strong hands violently push his hand downward as he raised it to bless the area with holy water. Although a very imposing figure—6' 4" tall and 200 pounds—Father Creger exited the premises with the admonition that they should have dealt with their situation years earlier. In short, Kaitlynn says he left a believer. That's also when the activity rapidly escalated.

As is the case with life, it must go on, and in the midst of difficult moments, there is also time for romance. Kaitlynn met and fell in love with a young man from Ireland named Brendan. While Kaitlynn was home coping with spiritual shenanigans, Brendan was off in Ireland, leaving the love of his life achingly lonely. "One night in June of 2000," she says,

> I fell asleep thinking how lonely I was without Brendan. I suddenly awoke to the presence of a hand rubbing my back. It was a gentle sort of rubbing, like whoever was doing it was trying to console me. It didn't work. I immediately arched my back out of fear and I felt the hand move away.

I guess it's hard to trust the sympathies of a ghost after

years of abuse of power on their part.

Kaitlynn has often felt the clasp of an unseen hand upon hers. On many occasions, however, it's the clasp of a hand upon her foot. "Once," she says,

> I was setting up my sleeping bag on the floor of my parents' bedroom getting ready for sleep. I reminded myself mentally that I needed to get up at 7 A.M. for 7:30 mass Sunday morning. At 7 A.M. on the dot I was awakened by a tug on my foot by an unseen hand. If that hadn't happened, I would have missed mass, so I think that at least this time that particular spirit was trying to be helpful.

It's almost always the bedrooms that are the most active rooms in the house, although the haunting spreads itself out over the entire abode. As recently as July of 2000, as Kaitlynn once again tried to catch up on her rest by lying on the floor of her sister's former bedroom, she looked up to see the face of an old man staring down upon her. "It was very clear," she says,

> and it wasn't anyone I had ever seen before. It was just the face and he was really old. It wasn't just a second or two, either, but every time I'd look up, there it would be, just staring at me. Finally, I got really scared and jumped up and ran out of the room. I was going to go downstairs to tell my mother what was going on, and as I passed by her bedroom, I could see another man sitting on her bed, looking over his shoulder at me. By that time, I was terrified and I ran downstairs and got my mother. We went back upstairs, but no one was there, which didn't surprise either of us very much. Later that month, my mother went to use the upstairs bathroom and, when she got to the doorway, she saw an old woman standing in there. We have no idea if these ghosts are connected to one another or not.

By now you've probably gotten the idea that Kaitlynn spends a lot of her slumber time out of her bedroom and on the floor of her parents' room, which she does. She is not, however, the only family member who prefers carpeting to mattresses—not out of convenience, but out of necessity. "I stopped sleeping in my bed, too," says Kerry.

When I still lived at home, I would have nights where this dark form would float into my room and above my bed. Sometimes it would hover by the foot of the bed. Then it would slide over the top of me and hold me down. Whenever that would happen, I felt like I couldn't breathe or scream or anything. I'd start thinking a prayer, and it would lighten up and eventually go away. I started sleeping on the floor to avoid it.

Sibling Mary has also had troubles with this dark entity. Only in her case, the spirit seemed to crawl into her room, then crawl up onto the bed and cover her with a great pressure. "Whenever it would happen," says Kaitlynn, speaking for her sister,

it would press the side of her head down hard against the pillow. Then it would start to bring its face down toward hers. She would make it go away by telling it to go back to hell where it came from. Since she has moved out, she has taken that spirit with her. It no longer plagues our house at all, but it's now in her apartment with her. She has a lot of stories of her own to tell about what goes on at her apartment.

As a result of my conversations with the haunted, I have become amazed at how many ghosts have an affinity for the bathroom. I don't know if these specters had poor plumbing facilities in their homes when they were part of the living, and are attracted to modern amenities, or if this is the fascination some ghosts seem to have with water itself. At any rate, nearly every haunted house I have visited has had ghosts in the "water closet," as the British are wont to say. Naturally, I just had to know if the house in Dearborn Heights experienced this same affinity. I was informed that they certainly had.

"The only room in the house where I always see a

ghost is the upstairs bathroom," says Kaitlynn. "Every single time I go in to use the bathroom, there is this man who stands off in the corner and watches me. Actually, no matter what reason I'm in there, he's in there, too."

I expressed to Kaitlynn how unfortunate this could be, seeing that the bathroom is the one room of the house that simply can't be avoided. She assured me of its inconvenience and tells me she tries not to look over in the corner where he is while she is in there. When I asked how in the world she could live with this on a daily basis, she told me that since it has taken place as long as she can remember, she is actually, in a weird sort of way, used to him being there. I know there are a good many people who have grown accustomed to the spirits in their homes, and I have been one of them. But invading the privacy of one's personal privy crosses the line of good taste for even the most ill-mannered of ghosts. The only advantage I can imagine would be that it would serve to shorten lengths of stay in there.

After having visited the Kennedy home, I shifted my attention to other haunted places on my paranormal menu. A few short days later, I received an e-mail from Kaitlynn, thanking me for my visit and my counsel and pointing out that since my visit, things really got stirred up around there. She wrote that two nights after I had left, she was awakened by the same presence she is normally plagued by and that she was once again pinned down on the floor, but this time not quite so violently. If I were her, I'm not certain I would have been thankful for any visit that stirred up what was already far too active, but such is the tone of her personality.

In the fall of 2001, Kaitlynn returned to Albion College for the beginning of her senior year. As expected, at least one evil entity packed its bags and returned to her apartment with her. "My roommate and I weren't the only ones in the apartment," she says.

There's a very scary presence that seemed to hang out around our couch. My roommate sensed it too, and it terrified her. I also had another bad experience while trying to sleep. I had fallen asleep and was dreaming about my fiancé, Brendan, and a home they have in Ireland. I dreamed I was walking through that house and that I was very frightened. I finally made myself wake up, which is something I can do when dreams like that plague me. As I awakened, I could sense a strong presence lying on the bed next to me. It spoke to me and told me I wasn't supposed to wake up yet, that I had to go back to sleep. I resisted and tried to open my eyes, but I felt its fingers over my eyelids, trying to push them down. I could hear its voice and feel its strength, although I can still not say what sex it was. I was forced to keep my eyes closed, and finally I fell back to sleep and actually finished the dream I had started earlier. In that dream I had an older woman come to me and guide me through the house I was in. The next day I called Brendan and told him about the dream. When I described the house, I was correct in my description, right down to the number of landings in the house and the presence of a cellar and an attic, which I did not know at the time were rarities in Ireland.

In May of 2002, Kaitlynn graduated from Albion College and quickly moved out to California to pursue a master's degree.

"Since I moved to California in order to pursue my master's in forensic science," she says,

I realized I had brought some spirits with me. For instance, my apartment always has a strange feel to it, and I've heard footsteps in the hallway and have seen fleeting images here and there. Our pots and pans rattle both whether they are in the drawers or on the stove.

It would appear to me that it would be difficult to keep roommates when ghosts pull pranks in the kitchen or run rampant in the hallways. Indeed, Kaitlynn's current roommate has enjoyed a few phantasmagorical displays of paranormal intrusions since moving in with her. "One night," says Kaitlynn,

> my roommate and I were studying together, so everything was naturally very quiet for about an hour. All of a sudden, a bottle of my nail polish went flying off the living room table across the room from us. It was just like someone had backhanded it really hard—it just flew across the room. It shook both of us up a bit. Not long after that, my roommate began seeing a woman, who we think is responsible for the nail polish and the shaking pans, standing in her bedroom, looking at her. She usually sees this woman when she wakes up in the middle of the night. I guess I'm not the only one of us who seems to be tuned in to these sorts of things.

It also appears the foot-tugging spirit back home drops in for a cross-country visit from time to time. On more than one occasion, Kaitlynn has been awakened by someone grabbing her feet and shaking them violently. It is so unsettling that she is unable to drift back to sleep. "Along with the interruptions of my sleep," she says,

> a lot of other strange things plague me. Sometimes I'll be asleep, and I'll be awakened by a noise. It's usually the sound of the things on my dresser being moved around. I'll lay there and listen, and it sounds just like someone is shifting everything around. While I hear the noise, I never see the movement of the items, nor do I see who is doing it.

While there are some who would claim all this phenomena can be easily explained away through the casual use of causal logic, there is one repetitive action that rather defies logical thought altogether. "Lots of times," says Kaitlynn,

> I'll be in bed and I'll hear someone tapping on my bedroom window. It isn't that faint kind of tapping that makes you wonder if you're really hearing something, it's a definite, attention getting tapping, like someone

is rapping on the glass with their knuckles.

What makes this difficult to dismiss is the fact that Kaitlynn's apartment is on the second floor, and her bedroom window in particular is not accessible without a ladder. "When I get up and look outside," she says,

> I don't see anything or anybody. There aren't even any tree branches nearby that could bump into the glass. This sort of thing makes you feel watched all the time and is especially unnerving in the middle of the night.

It appears poor Kaitlynn has nowhere to run where ghosts are concerned. They bother her at home and they tag along when she goes away. They intrude on her privacy and they are rude to her friends. They pester her parents and they undauntedly terrorize her elder siblings. Ask her what her most frightening moments have been, and there are simply too many of them for her memory to sort through. The best she can do is refer to the most frightening recent experience. "My scariest moment out here in California was last week," she asserts (June of 2002).

> I was home from classes on my lunch break, and decided I needed a nap to catch up on all the sleep I've lost to these horrible intrusions. I had probably been sleeping for only a few minutes, when I woke up with the blankets over the top of my head—which isn't unusual for me, because I learned I had to sleep this way when I was a little girl. Anyway, I woke up to the noise of heavy footsteps. I could tell they were starting from the side of my bed near my desk. Then they went up to the head of my bed and continued to the side where I was lying. Then they stopped, and I heard whoever it was start to whistle. At first I thought it was Amy, my roommate, but I knew she wouldn't do that to me while I was sleeping, so then I thought maybe someone had broken in to the apartment. Then it suddenly got on top of me, and I felt this sharp electric shock go all through my body. Then my bed started shaking, so finally I fought against it and managed to sit up. When I did, and I looked around, there wasn't

anyone in the room—or in the apartment for that matter. I was all alone.

To fully respect the intensity of fear Kaitlynn felt during this horrifying escapade, remember that she purposefully visits death sites and attends autopsies as a part of her graduate training in forensics. That alone would terrify most of us, perhaps even traumatize us to the point of no mental return. If this soul can persevere those macabre settings, then her clashes with vengeful spirits must rate a ten on the Richter Scale.

Naturally I inquired as to the effect death scenarios and autopsy visitations have on her. In short, I wanted to know if anything strange ever occurred during these settings. "I attended a suicide scene," she says,

> as a part of my internship. While such an event is sort of unsettling, and it's natural to be put off by it a bit at first, the investigation work that goes into it is fascinating. The next day, though, I was in my apartment getting ready to go out for the evening, and I saw something out of the corner of my eye. When I looked over toward my bedroom, I saw a man standing in my bedroom doorway, looking at me. It was the same man who had committed suicide, whose death I had help investigate as part of my training. Now that's a bit unusual, I'd say.

As for autopsies, Kaitlynn had this to say:

> My internship involves several trips to the morgue. I have found that, although it's interesting, it's extremely difficult for me to do. I have to force myself to attend. The moment I get to the morgue with the others, the air gets very heavy and I start to feel pressure on my body. After the sessions are over, I feel drained when I leave that place. I think that's what scares me the most about connecting with the spirits of the dead who are trying to come through. The fear is overwhelming, and the intense physical pressure I feel is overbearing. It's frightening to feel like all your energy is being sucked out of your body. After a training session at the morgue, all I can do is go home

and lie down, I'm too exhausted for anything else. At the same time, I am more and more aware of my psychic abilities and that assures me I have chosen the correct field to go into. I hope to do death scene investigations as a career, and I guess my abilities will allow me to take my work to the next level.

Indeed.

When one considers the intensity of the hauntings recorded in this frightening tale, as well as the location of the home and the participation of all the females within the household, one must pause to reflect a while. Does the proximity of the home in Dearborn Heights to the cemetery it abuts figure into the bizarre displays of paranormal activity? Are Kaitlynn, her mother, and her sisters all gifted with an unusually high degree of psychic sensitivity? Is the house some sort of conduit for spiritual entering and exiting? Could all of these questions be answered in the affirmative? Perhaps it truly is a combination of spirits being drawn to a particular place, in this case the Kennedy family homestead, because the house sits in a sensitive area and is inhabited by sensitive people. Consider what follows.

As a rule, I almost never consult a psychic. In fact, the only ones I have made contact with are the ones who have first gotten ahold of me. Even when I do entertain the input of a person who purports to be psychically gifted, I usually put them to a small test or two to assure myself they aren't just blowing the proverbial ethereal smoke in my face. And if a gifted soul agrees to participate in my questioning, I make it clear I do not provide remuneration for such talents offered.

Enter Melissa Cofer-Jones, a sincere and kind young woman residing in Jackson, Michigan. After sending me an e-mail complimenting the efforts of my first book, I replied back electronically. She didn't impose herself upon me and that was endearing to me. On the other hand, I risked being seen as rude by asking her if I could put her to the test concerning a home that was experiencing an intense haunting. That home was the Kennedy house in Dearborn Heights. My conversation with Melissa at this point was over the phone; we had never met or spoken to one another previously. When I asked if she could read the home, all she asked for was the address, which I supplied her. I didn't tell her anything about the home, the haunting, or the fine folks involved. All Melissa received from me was the address.

Melissa grew quiet for a moment, and I, on the other end of the line, sipped my tea like a good Scotsman ought in mid-afternoon. Then, Melissa began to speak. She said she sensed great anger and hostility coming from the spirits in the house, that they weren't there to watch out for the residents or to seek out their help. They were instead openly hostile to them. She maintained there were several entities within those walls, and that one of them appears as a relative. Then she said,

> There's something about the land. I'm picking up that this family built the home, and when they bought the land they were lied to. They were told their lot was not a part of an original cemetery nearby, a cemetery that was eventually relocated. In fact, I'm picking up that it was part of it. And I'm also picking up that there's an Indian involved in this somehow, that perhaps an old Indian burial mound was disturbed when the property was developed years ago. The house is on a spot we call a portal, an area where spirits are drawn to. And most of the family members are really sensitive to spirits and pick up on everything around them.

I thanked Melissa for her time, and then contacted the Kennedy family. When I listed the individual things Melissa had told me, confirmation on all of them was forthcoming. Indeed, the Kennedys assert that they were lied to about the building lot they had purchased, as they asked the seller if it had ever been a part of the cemetery and he had told them it hadn't. They maintain they found out later that it had. As to the Indian,

Kaitlynn said,

> Oh, yes. I forgot about that. One of the first ghosts I ever encountered was that of an old Indian man. Later, while digging a garden in our yard, we found a lot of Indian arrowheads and things.

Right on, Melissa.

As if this weren't enough, I phoned another woman who seems to have interesting paranormal gifts. I told her only general information about the activity of the home, and she agreed to drive by and see if she could sense anything unusual there. I shall call this woman Kristen. Kristen phoned me later and said,

> Yes, that house is bad. I parked outside across the street one afternoon and just looked over at it. My impression is that there's a lot of things going on in there. I sense that a lot of the spirits from the cemetery behind it pass through the house. But there's scarier stuff than that going on in there. There are beings in there that aren't human.

When my ears heard the words "aren't human," I snapped to full attention, and asked her to explain. "There are very negative entities in there," replied Kristen.

> They are drawn to the ground the house is on because it's a portal [there's that word again] for spirits crossing over. They also hate the fact that the residents are very religious and practice their religion faithfully. It won't be easy to remove these negative entities from the house.

Kristen then went on to tell me that I had visited the house on one occasion. I confessed that I had, but I told her that, curiously, I had sensed nothing, and felt perfectly comfortable in the house even though my hosts were frightened all the while I was there. I told her that, to me, the house seemed quite normal. "That's because of who you are," replied Kristen.

> You are an ordained minister. They are afraid of you,

and though they hate it when you come around, they stay hidden out of fear of you. In fact, when I was across the street looking at the house, I could see your first visit there.

I then asked Kristen what she saw, and what she had to say prompted me to stiffen my tea with a little blended Scottish support. She asked, "Did you get the feeling that something was stalking you, that some creature was standing very near to you, circling you?" I replied that I had no such sensation. "Well," she said,

it certainly was. I could see you in the foyer, when you first came in [incidentally, she was able to describe the interior of the home nearly perfectly], it grew very apprehensive, and circled you around and around, sniffing at your neck. It wasn't human and had cloven feet and a snout like a dog, although it stood on two legs. There's more than one of these negative creatures in there, but they're afraid of you and won't show themselves while you're around—but after you leave, they really start to give the family a hard time.

If such creatures truly exist, I'm just as glad my ordination keeps them at bay. I'm normally pretty brave in the face of apparitional shenanigans, but I really don't have any desire to confront a half dog, half who-knows-what as it sniffs and snorts in nasty indignation. Even I have enough sense to draw the line somewhere.

Well, as with all chapters in this book, this marathon tale must now come to a close. I admit this is one doozy of a haunting and perhaps one of the three most overtly haunted places I have ever visited—at least as far as private dwellings are concerned. And as I close this chapter, the chapter is really not closed at all on the haunted Kennedy home in Dearborn Heights.

4

Pull up a Chair and Make Yourself Comfortable / The Gang's All Here

Location of Haunting: The Olympia Bookstore is located at 208 S. Front Street, in downtown Dowagiac, Michigan. Coming from the eastern part of the state, take I-94 west until you're just getting a bit tired of freeway driving. Say farewell to the expressway at exit 56, which is Highway 51 South. Follow 51 south through the town of Decatur and continue along to Dowagiac. Eventually you must choose to turn either right or left. Opt for the right (which will still be 51) and immediately turn left onto Front Street. The Olympia Bookstore is just down the way a bit.

If coming from the Chicago area, get on the Indiana Turnpike (I-80/I-90) headed eastward. Exit at Highway 31 and steer north. Get off on US-12 and head east into Niles, Michigan. In Niles get on 51 and go north once again. This route will take you into Dowagiac; as you approach the downtown area, look for Front Street on your right. Ah, how refreshing to provide fellow ghost afficionados the exact location of a haunted dwelling!

Period of Haunting: It is difficult to say when the apparitions began skittering about the shelves of this bookstore. Although previous owners of the building have not confessed to any abnormalities between the walls, the present owner, Paul Pugh, as well as many of his friends, relatives, and customers, insist the aberrant behaviors have gone on for many years now. Paul has been the sole proprietor of the Olympia since 1987 and insists the haunting began soon after he set up shop.

Date of Investigation: My first contact with Paul Pugh was by telephone in the summer of 2001, at the suggestion of a resident of the area, Jody Crandall of the Coloma High School Library. Her referral came about as a result of having read an interview I gave to the *Detroit Free Press*. In contacting me about the Olympia Bookstore, she referred to the entity there as "a gentleman ghost." Well, it's nice to know that some ghosts maintain a sense of dignity as they invade our space—or as we invade theirs. An extensive interview, resulting in this story and generating a lead for another Dowagiac haunting, took place in mid-July of 2002.

Description of Location: The shop at 208 S. Front is one of the original structures within the limits of the city. Dowagiac is one of the oldest settlements in Michigan and was a way station for railroads between Detroit and Chicago. Prior to the railroads, it was a stopover for early settlers heading west by horse, wagon, and on foot. It is a beautiful city, and its citizens are quite proud of the area. Each summer, a major street fair celebrating the arts takes place, drawing artisans and literary notables from all over the country. On that literary note, Paul Pugh has informed me that Dowagiac was the last place visited by Joseph Heller, author of *Catch-22*, before his recent death, and that he has also had the opportunity to share a glass of whiskey with Kurt Vonnegut, who penned, among other famous works, *Slaughterhouse Five*. If you're unfamiliar with these authors and their modern-day classics, then perhaps you've been reading too many trashy ghost stories and could benefit from the conscience-tweaking prose of these artistic giants.

The Olympia Bookstore is typical of the original

structures of its day and dates back to at least the 1850s. It is an elongated, narrow two-story structure, with the bookstore spreading out its wares on the main floor and rented living quarters stretching out above. The entry to the retail section of the building is recessed, and the access to the upper residential section is to the immediate right of it. This building has served many purposes throughout its long history, having been home to a drugstore, a buggy repair and sales establishment, and, for a short while in the late 1800s, a funeral home, just to name a few. If appearance alone determined whether or not a place was haunted, then, in my estimation, the Olympia Bookstore would certainly qualify as being host to an entity or two.

The Haunt Meter: * * ½ (downstairs) * * * * (upstairs)

Part One:
Pull up a Chair and
Make Yourself Comfortable

Paul Pugh is amiable and soft spoken. He has dealt in fine books for over forty years and is a good resource for someone desiring to know the whereabouts of a particular edition or the worth of a particular printing. Prior to moving to Dowagiac, he earned his living as a book dealer in Indiana. Savvy to the possibilities of Internet retailing, he says the bulk of his business is done online and that the store itself is open only two days a week—usually Tuesdays and Fridays—or by appointment. Such is the age in which we live, when customers would rather mouse-click their way through a seller's wares than pore over the bookshelves in person, soaking in the cultural ambiance and delighting in the sights and smells of the musty manuscripts themselves. Ah, progress!

Paul was quite patient with my inquiries into his personal and professional space as my questions delved more and more into his encounters with the spirits of his establishment. In fact, he is rather open to sharing his experiences. "The first thing I noticed as being odd," says Paul,

> was when I would come to the building in the morning to open up. There were times when I'd approach the front door and there would be a chair pulled up in front of the door on the inside. It was positioned in such a way that it looked like someone had dragged it over to the door so they could sit and watch what was going on outside at night. I'd put the chair back where it belonged and usually it would stay there several days. Then I'd find it back in front of the doorway again. I sort of got used to that—and it still happens from time to time. I do have to admit, though, that the first couple times it happened I felt a little freaked out. Now, though, I don't have any apprehensions about being in the store alone.

It appears obvious that the ghost of the Olympia likes to make himself comfortable and rest his weary soul while surveying the nocturnal activities of the town, but I wanted to know if he was active during the daylight hours as well. "Yes," says Paul,

> we have things that go on during the day quite a bit. Lots of times I'll be working and I'll hear the sound of books being slid across a shelf—that's a sound that's unmistakable in this business. I used to go and look around whenever I heard it, but now I know it's just the ghost. Besides, nothing is ever really moved when I hear that sound, and I'm not the only one to hear it. Customers and friends have been here when it's happened.

While strange sounds seem to permeate the business, the movements seem to take place after closing hours, as with the chair incidents. "There are also times when I'll open up in the morning and find some books scattered out on the floor. There's no way they could have fallen. It's more like someone had taken them and dropped them there," he says. This makes me wonder if whoever is pulling up a chair is also feeding their intellectual and artistic curiosities with the plethora of books all around him—sort of like locking an avid reader in a library.

I have repeatedly referred to this ghost as "he," and with good reason. Paul believes the ghost is a man. In fact, Paul has given the ghostly resident a name. "We call him 'Mr. Bock'," says Paul, whose use of the formal title signifies proper respect for his disembodied guest. "We got that name from the stairwell that goes up to the apartment. Obviously, a Mr. C. E. Bock once lived there, although no one in town seems to recall anyone by that name."

A few years ago, Paul divided the main floor area into two sections and rented out one of them to a woman named Kay Smith who runs a frame shop there. There is an open doorway between the two businesses, giving customers of either shop the ability to move back and forth without having to go outside. "Kay has had a few experiences of her own," says Paul.

> She has heard the books as they've been shuffled around on the shelves, but the haunting seems to express itself mostly on my side of the building. However, Kay has a buzzer on the front entrance to her frame shop. It's the kind where you have to go through the door and break a beam to set off the buzzer. She installed it so she would know when someone came in if she was working out back. Anyway, there have been times when I'd be working alone after closing time in the bookstore, and I'd hear the buzzer go off on Kay's side. I'd go over to see who had come in, but every time it happened the door would be closed and locked, and no one would be over there.

I asked Paul if, amongst all the strangeness of his shop, he has ever seen a ghost skulking about the bookshelves. "No," he says, "that sort of thing doesn't go on down here. You have to go upstairs for that." Apparently, the haunting on the main floor is nothing compared to the actions of the wayward ghosts up above. So, dear reader, let's exit the Olympia Bookstore and head up the front stairway to the apartment above, where things seem to be a tad more sporting, to say the least.

Part Two:
The Gang's All Here

"If you really want to talk about a haunted place," Paul says, "you need to explore the apartment." He then went on to refer me to one of the former residents of the apartment upstairs, Lacy Ignacio-Gunn, a vivacious and multi-talented young woman of twenty-six who lived in the apartment for a few years and whose father still resides there.

"I lived there for three years, from 1998 through 2000," Lacy says.

> And there was stuff happening up there on a daily basis. It's a strangely laid out apartment. It's sort of narrow, but really long, and it's over 1,800 square feet. There's a bedroom in front, and a bedroom in back, and rooms in between. There's one long hallway that runs the length of the building, and you can see down that hallway from front to back. The only windows are in the front bedroom, looking out onto Front Street, and the ones off in the back bedroom, so there's not a lot of natural light going in the place. I guess there's about six rooms including the bathroom and one pretty large closet, too.

I asked Lacy about any ghostly activity. "Where do I start?" she muses.

> Well, first of all, let me say that my dad and I have

always been involved in community theater, and our apartment was where everybody involved with the theater would congregate after rehearsals and shows. It wasn't very often that just my dad and I would spend the night there. There would always be eight to twelve people over, just visiting or spending the night. Most of the weird stuff was witnessed by everyone.

When I asked Lacy if she meant that more than one person at a time would witness the ghostly antics, she said, "Yes, most of the time the whole group of us would see and hear things."

It isn't often that there are group sightings of strange phenomena, so I encouraged Lacy to continue. "There would be a group of us at the apartment," she went on to say,

and we would hear the downstairs door open and then the sound of footsteps coming up. Someone would say, "here comes so and so," thinking another friend was on the way up. When no one would come through the door, we'd think maybe someone was playing a prank on us, so we'd look down the stairway and there wouldn't be anyone there. But that doesn't just happen in the evening when there are lots of people visiting, it happens every day, sometimes several times a day. It's a common event. I'd be alone there during the day, and I'd hear it all the time. I'd check to make sure the door was locked, and it would still happen, morning, noon, and night. My dad hears it a lot, too.

Lacy's dad, John Ignacio, is a forty-eight-year-old professional, employed at a local zinc processing plant. He is also involved in community theater with his daughter.

"My dad and I always had lots of people over spending the night," says Lacy.

One of the strange things that we can't explain is how we'd all be asleep and, say about 3 A.M. or so, we'd all suddenly wake up within about thirty seconds of one another. We'd jump up and just naturally migrate to the living room. Someone would nervously say, "let's go get ice cream," or "let's go outside for awhile," and off we'd go. That happened a lot while I was there. It was like we all knew something was waking us up, but we didn't know why and we really didn't want to talk about it.

As I noted earlier, most ghosts usually don't make their presence known when there is a group of people milling about. The ghosts of this residence are the exception. "To give you an example of how active these ghosts are," says Lacy,

we had a lot of house guests over one evening, which wasn't new for us, and we were sitting around wondering what to do, to go to the movies or stay in and play a game. There must have been at least ten of us, and everybody was trying to make up their mind. Well, there's a really big closet off the living room, and among other things we keep our games in there. The door to the closet is really hard to open because my dad ran the cable to the TV under the closet door so it would be out of the way. In order to open the door you have to give it a real hard tug so it can go over the cable. Anyway, we decided to stay in and play a game, but we were sort of arguing over which one to play. We finally decided, but we were all too lazy to get up and get it out of the closet. Finally, one of my friends said, "I'll get it!" and started for the closet. Before he even got there, the closet door just swung open all by itself, with no effort whatsoever. It was so out of the realm of normal possibility that some of my friends actually started screaming and others just stared in disbelief. A couple of them had been skeptics up until then, but that converted them instantly. Finally, we sort of laughed it off and went ahead with our game.

Living in a haunted house has got to have its share of disconcerting moments, so I asked Lacy if she had been comfortable living there. "For the most part I was," she says.

But you have to realize that I was hardly ever alone there. The mood could change, though. When I was alone there, things would start to happen—you know, the strong sense that you weren't alone—and then the negative feelings would build up stronger and stronger until you didn't know how much longer you could stand it in there. If you stayed in control of yourself, you'd be all right. But that was almost impossible for me to do. The strong presence of the spirits would become overpowering and I'd feel surrounded and suffocated. It would be all through the apartment and you couldn't get rid of it. That's when I would really start to feel overwhelmed and I'd have to get out of there as fast as I could because of the intense fear. I'd go visit a friend or something and they'd understand, because they could sense the spirits whenever they would visit.

"I remember once," she says,

when my friend Joanne stayed over for the night. Normally we would sleep in separate bedrooms, but all that evening we just kept getting the weird sensation that we weren't alone, that someone was watching us. We started out in separate bedrooms, but pretty soon we shared a bed in the back bedroom. We fell asleep, and a short while later I woke up to see this figure of a person standing between my side of the bed and the closet, which meant it was standing right next to my head because there's not much room between the bed and the closet. I think it was a man because it was wearing a long overcoat and a fedora. All I could do was stare at it, I was so scared. I didn't know if Joanne was awake, so I just reached over and grabbed hold of her and pulled her up to a sitting position. What's interesting is that Joanne had awakened at the same moment I had, and she had been watching this thing, too. We must have sat there, staring at it, for at least five minutes, but it felt more like a long half hour. We couldn't move, we were so out of it. We just sat there with our hands over our mouths. He looked to be huge, at least six-feet tall, which is pretty huge if you're only five-foot-two like me. He never moved, but just stood there watching us. Then, all of a sudden, he was just gone.

I asked Lacy how she reacted to her intruder when it was all over. "Are you kidding? We got out of that bedroom and slept together on the couch with the TV going and the lights on!" Not an unreasonable response considering the conditions.

It would appear the ghost in the tasteful fedora, as well as the playful spirit who wanted to join in on board game night, aren't the only otherworldly entities prowling about the rental property. "I like children a lot," says Lacy.

> Children and animals are dear to me, and they seem to be attracted to me, too. I can be at the supermarket, and kids I've never seen before will walk up to me and start up a conversation. I think maybe it's the same with ghosts who are children, because I'm almost certain one of the ghosts in the apartment is a little child.

When I asked Lacy what made her think this, she said,

> Because there are times when some of the things that happen up there are things a child would do. When I lived there, I'd sometimes come home to find the big closet open, and some of the games would be set on the floor, like someone was going through them. They hadn't fallen off the shelves, it always looked like they'd been strewn out over the floor like someone would do when they were trying to make up their mind what to play with. A child would put them on the floor, an adult wouldn't. And not only that, but there would be times when I'd go into the kitchen and the cookies would be out of the cupboard and laying on the counter. When these things would happen, I'd get the strong impression there was a young child nearby. It wasn't a scary feeling.

The ghosts of the haunted apartment in Dowagiac are diverse in nature. Sometimes they are subtle, often they are obtuse, sometimes they are invasive. All in all, they prove to be an eclectic mix of ectoplasmic delights.

(Actually, there is no ectoplasma involved with this story, but the phrase does sound catchy, doesn't it?) "There are times," says Lacy,

> when you can tell the ghosts are there, but you're pretty much okay with it—as long as someone's there with you. Once, a friend and I were sitting on the couch watching TV. From where you are on the couch, you can see down the hall all the way to the back of the apartment. While we were watching, a ghost just crossed over through the hallway. I said to my friend, "Did you see that?" and she said, "Yeah." Then we just went back to watching our show. That sort of thing happened all the time, and lots of people have experienced it.

Evidently, the ghosts feel slighted by too much television watching and not enough attention given to them. Not only do they flit through the hallway, interrupting one's concentration on a program, but they play with the television set itself. "My dad, after I moved out and he was living there alone, told me of some trouble he had one night with the TV," Lacy recalls.

> He was in another room and he heard the television going. He knew he hadn't turned it on, so he went in to the living room to investigate. As he stood there trying to figure out what was going on, the channels started to change all by themselves and the power started going on and off. He looked for the remote and found it lying on the coffee table where it belonged. Whatever was doing it, it wasn't the remote. But these things don't seem to bother him like they bother me.

Quite often, it's possible to tell if your abode is running amok with spirits by simply watching your pets. For some reason, animals seem to sense—if not hear, smell, and see—ghosts. Usually, they don't care for the experience and they will behave erratically or angrily in their presence. Then again, maybe it's the ghosts who don't like the pets, and I shouldn't be so quick to pin the rap on the animals. No matter. If you think your house may be host to a spirit or two, sit quietly and watch your cat or dog as it roams the premises. In Lacy's case, she watched her cats. "When I lived there with my dad," she says,

> we had some cats. They'd really freak out when the ghosts were around, which was most of the time. Sometimes, they'd be sleeping on the couch and all of a sudden they'd jump up and run toward the front door, like they heard someone coming up the stairs. Then they'd crouch down and back up, snarling and hissing. They'd start looking up just the way they would if someone were walking toward them. Judging from the angle, it looked like whoever they were watching was about five foot eight to five foot ten.

I wonder, could the Mr. Bock whose name is written on the stairwell wall fit that description? If so, perhaps he was not a lover of felines.

"There would be times," continues Lacy,

> when I'd be playing fetch with the cats, and I would throw a ball for them to chase. Well, they would chase it, but they rarely brought it back to you. Anyway, lots of times they'd run after the ball and jump on it, except for when I would throw the ball toward the front door. They'd run up towards the door, and then just stop dead in their tracks. They would refuse to go near that door.

Lacy didn't leave the apartment because of the ghosts, but for far more romantic reasons. She married Jeff, who by the time of their marriage was well acquainted with the activity up on that second floor. Until they could secure a place of their own, they took up temporary residence in the apartment's back bedroom.

"There's a deck outside the back bedroom," says Lacy.

> It was nice to sit out there on hot summer nights. But one night, it had been really storming outside when we went to bed. As Jeff told me after this event, he drifted awake and just lay there for a minute or two listening

to the storm outside. He said that as he lay there, the door that goes out to the deck just flew open—and that's a door we always checked every night before we went to bed and we kept it deadbolted. Just about that time, he said I jumped out of bed and headed toward that door, saying, "He wants me to come with him." Jeff could tell I was asleep at the time and he was really freaking out. I guess I went right out the door and onto the deck, with the rain pouring down all over me. By this time, he's screaming at me and shaking me. I finally woke up, and Jeff told me what I said. I was still half asleep when I said, "Oh, you're talking about Bob." Then Jeff led me back to bed and we talked about what had happened. I know the only way the name Bob came to me was because I was still half asleep. I don't have any idea who he is, but he sure had a hold on me.

Isn't it refreshing to run into a ghost with an ordinary old name like "Bob"? It sort of makes you wonder just how nasty any ghost with that moniker could be. Maybe he just wanted to share the beauty of a summer storm with a charming young lady. Or maybe Bob is just shy and can only express the nature of his infatuation with Lacy while she's semi-conscious.

At least one ghost on the premises appears to be protective by nature. This next story is not only an example of protectiveness, but perhaps an indication of how they can alter time and space to suit their—and our—needs. This nugget involves Lacy's father. It seems John suffers from sleep apnea, which may not be surprising considering what he has to live with day in and day out. At any rate, John was alone in the apartment when he had some sort of sleep-related physiological attack. He awakened terribly short of breath and immediately climbed out of bed, afraid he couldn't get his wind back. He looked at the digital clock on his night stand, which displayed a time of 2:34 A.M. For several nerve-wracking minutes he thought he was in serious physical trouble, but slowly his breathing returned to normal again. A little nervous about going immediately back to bed, he decided to engage himself in some channel surfing and went into the living room to watch television. A couple of programs later he climbed back into bed and fell asleep. Once again, he awakened suddenly. He didn't know why, but it wasn't because of his sleep disorder because he was breathing just fine. He looked over at the digital clock again, and it shone forth the time of 2:32 A.M.—two minutes before the attack he already had at 2:34 A.M.! Understandably, this scared him more than just a little, and he decided sleep was no longer a priority that night.

The next day, Lacy came over to visit her father, and he related the incident to her, knowing that hers would be compassionate and understanding ears. Lacy offered the theory that one of the ghosts of the house had thrown her father backward in time when he had returned to bed, and then awakened him prior to 2:34 A.M. so that he would not experience the life threatening breathing episode. She said, "Dad, I think someone's watching out for you." The moment those words exited her lips, all the lights in the kitchen dimmed for a few seconds, and then went back up to normal brightness, as if giving approval of her theory. "We just stood there and shook our heads," says Lacy.

Before marrying Jeff, Lacy eventually decided she no longer enjoyed staying alone in the apartment. Whenever possible, which was nearly always, she invited guests over, not only for the evening, but for the night. "It reached a point where I didn't want to be alone in there anymore," she says.

> I was never alone in the first place because of the ghosts, but that's different. I made up my mind never to sleep there alone, because you would always hear footsteps going up and down the length of the hallway, or up the stairs from the street entry. I had to have someone with me or I'd have gone crazy.

Friends had no second thoughts about spending the night with Lacy. But it's interesting to note that almost all of her friends are involved in the community theater with her. It's been my experience that while creative, artistic folk are not only overly subject to paranormal encounters, they are less intimidated by ghostly activity than most people. Many of her friends found it entertaining to spend the night there and were fascinated to be a part of a genuine, one hundred percent, dyed-in-the-wool haunting—especially the type you could share as a group on an otherwise boring evening.

One particular night, after deep conversation about the spirits who seemed to roam the place at will, a group of Lacy's friends gathered in the living room in a concerted effort to make contact with the ghostly crew who hung out there. They broke out a Ouija board—something I find genuinely distasteful—and began their seance session. "We had just started using the board," says Lacy,

> and all of a sudden we could hear a sound byte from the computer off in the front bedroom. It was Homer Simpson's voice repeating a phrase he liked to use, saying over and over again, "Sixty-four slices of American Cheese on the wall." It kept repeating itself over and over. We all heard it plain as could be, and a couple of us ran in there. We could still hear it playing through the computer, but the computer was definitely off. We went back into the living room and it stopped, so we started using the Ouija again. As we did, a rush of air flew through the living room and blew out all the candles. That's when we decided it was a good idea to stop.

Well, there you have it, dear reader. A couple of truly entertaining haunts from the city of Dowagiac, both of which inhabit the same building. Jaunt on over some time and check out the Olympia Bookstore for yourself, but check first to see if it's going to be open. Fight off the impulse to embarrass yourself by wandering among the shelves all bug-eyed, in hopes of encountering an apparition or two. It is a place of business, you know, and the least you should do is respect it as such. So, buy a book first, and feel justified in perusing through the shelves all bug-eyed and hopeful. As for the apartment upstairs, it's a private residence, so it's best to keep your paws off the doorknob. They already have enough strange footsteps treading that stairway.

5

Center Stage
with the Ghosts

Location of Haunting: The Beckwith Theatre Company is a community theater located in downtown Dowagiac, in extreme southwestern Michigan. It is but a short minute's walk from the Olympia Bookstore, the subject of the previous chapter.

Period of Haunting: This dwelling, once a Methodist church, then a Knights of Columbus Hall (there's ecumenicalism for you), has been a community theater for over thirteen years. Those associated with the theater insist it has been haunted the entire time. It would not be a stretch to assume the haunting pre-dates its theater days.

Date of Investigation: The lead for this haunted place was given to me by Paul Pugh and Lacy Ignacio-Gunn when I spoke to them about the haunted bookstore and apartment in Dowagiac. That series of conversations took place in July of 2002.

Description of Location: The theater is a beautiful brick structure, the backside of which sports an oval shape, as that area was once the altar area of the church that initially inhabited the building. It is strikingly preserved and well-maintained. It consists of one floor and a basement. The former altar area was a natural for the placement of the stage when it became a theater.

The Haunt Meter: * * * *

While speaking with Paul Pugh, owner of the Olympia Bookstore, he said to me, "If you really want to experience some ghosts, you need to check out the Beckwith Theatre." When I asked who to contact, he chuckled a bit and directed me to Lacy Ignacio-Gunn, who figures strongly in the chapter concerning Paul's haunted upstairs apartment.

Lacy Ingnacio-Gunn is the executive director of the Beckwith Theatre Company. A young, energetic woman, she is devoted to acting and directing for the theater she serves. Lacy has been involved with the Beckwith for about half of the thirteen years it has been in existence, and she is more than enthusiastic about the productions offered therein, be they comedies, dramas, or musicals.

When I asked Lacy how active the spirits were in the theater she treasures, she exclaimed, "Oh, man! It's constant—there are tons of stories about this place." I didn't need to prod her on, as she was more than willing to share the chilling events with me. "There have been times," she says,

> when I've been alone in the theater and suddenly heard my name called out. I would be downstairs and it would sound like whoever called me was upstairs. Just about the time I would start to reply back, I would hear singing coming from upstairs. Not just one voice, but a whole bunch of voices. Usually I wouldn't be able to tell what they were singing because it was muffled, but it would definitely be singing going on. But the voice of who called my name would always be loud and crystal clear. The first couple of times that happened I would run up to see who was in the auditorium, but it would be dark and empty, and the noise would stop about the time I got to the top of the stairway.

I asked if it was a man or woman who was calling her name out, and she said it was different every time.

"Since I'm the executive director, I get to spend a great deal of time in the building, a lot of it all alone except for the spirits," says Lacy.

It's really difficult to remember a time when I wasn't alone in there, even when I was supposed to be. Nearly everybody who is involved in a production, whether they are support staff, actors, musicians, or even custodians, has had an experience with a ghost. And the sightings are multiple—I mean, there will be several of us together when things happen, like voices singing and having your name called out, or when you see an apparition.

These encounters with the spirits of the dead run the gamut of ethereal expression. "I think the most aggravating thing that happens to me is something that goes on continually," says Lacy.

I'll go into the building alone to work on something, and I'll carefully put my keys away. When I finish with what I'm doing, I'll reach for my keys and they'll be gone. That's when I find myself having to hunt all over the building until I find them. It's a huge key ring, and there are tons of keys on it, so there's no way you can miss them if they're anywhere near by. But they are never where I left them. Sometimes, and usually quite often, I'll find them in the men's restroom, an area of the building I don't exactly need to frequent. Other times I discover them in the kitchen, which is in a completely different part of the basement from where I'll be working. I've even found them upstairs on the stage when I hadn't even been upstairs. When it first started happening, I would get really scared. But now I think that the ghosts are just being playful. But it's the kind of playing around that makes extra work for me, and aggravates me. It's reached the point where I now have to plan to leave ten minutes earlier than necessary if I have somewhere to go, just so I'll have time to look for my keys.

I asked Lacy why she doesn't chastise the ghost who playfully absconds with her key ring and demand that it either leave them alone and find something more helpful to do, or give her some help in finding them once they've been purloined. She replied, "I guess I could do that, I never thought of it before." Then I suggested that maybe the ghost who does this isn't being playful, but is trying for some reason to get her attention, and that maybe she should try to discover what the ghost wants. Again, Lacy indicated she hadn't thought of that explanation and assured me she would give it some thought.

Lacy isn't the only one to be musically entertained by the creative ghosts of Beckwith Theatre. "There's usually a lot of activity in the building," she says.

> You know, people hang around after rehearsals and shows. We usually congregate in the basement and talk and get loud. One time in particular, there was a group of about twelve of us down there after a rehearsal. All of a sudden we heard singing coming from upstairs. We all stopped what we were doing and looked sort of wide-eyed at each other. The singing was coming from up in the auditorium, and it was a tune from *Godspell*, you know, "Day by Day." We could actually make out the tune and hear the words. It sounded like a whole chorus. Some of us headed up there, but by the time we got part way up the stairs, it had stopped. When we looked in the auditorium, it was like a tomb. Now, how do you deny something like that when so many people all heard it together?

It seems that the ghosts wandering about the place like to wait until the cast and crew are down in the basement before they break out in song. "After one night's performance," says Lacy,

> a lot of us hung out downstairs like we always do. After a while, we could hear the piano playing upstairs in the auditorium. Then, after a moment or two, we all heard someone start to sing along with the piano. We must have listened for three or four minutes before we decided to go take a look. Of course, it stopped just before we got up there. It always does.

I've suggested to Lacy that perhaps the ghosts are auditioning, in hopes of landing a part in an upcoming production. Perhaps she and her crew should simply stay down in the basement while the ghosts played and sang, then offer polite applause and encouragement. I pointed out that I would hesitate to express constructive criticism, as who wants to suffer the possible wrath of a spirit scorned?

I found it intriguing that the singing seems to correlate with the historical functions of the building. That is to say, now that it's a theater, the ghosts break out in songs from popular musicals. But at least one time the singing seemed to come from another era in the building's history. "One time a bunch of us were downstairs," says Lacy, "and we could hear singing coming again from upstairs. We listened close and we could tell that they were singing old hymns." Could it be the spirits of the former congregation are still practicing for the choir? Is it really a gathering of ghosts waxing religious for us? Or is it more like a time warp, where voices once raised in song are now drifting back down again for the edification of another generation? It's hard to tell. But if they're playing the piano, you can bet it's not the one they tuned up with decades ago, as it's long gone to the junkyard by now.

Production time around the Beckwith is often frenzied, especially on nights of the performances. Actors and directors and stagehands scurry about, all trying feverishly to do their jobs so that everything goes off without a hitch. Costume changes are being made, actors are touching up their makeup, and set designers race to set up the next scene. "It's a madhouse of activity downstairs during a show," says Lacy.

> You'll be trying to do your job, and people will be shooting past you constantly. Then when you expect it least, you'll see someone go flying by who doesn't belong there. That happens to us a lot, I'd say fifty percent of the time. And I'm not the only one to see the

ghost flit past. Others will look at me and say, "Did you see that?" and I'll just shake my head and try to move things along. It's really fascinating how actively involved the ghosts are with what we're doing in there.

The ghosts of the Beckwith aren't merely into acting, they are fascinated with interacting. Unafraid to make their presence known, they often go to extreme, if not outright silly, measures to be noticed. "This one is really good," says Lacy.

One night there was a bunch of us guys down in the basement. It was getting kind of late, but we were all in a pretty good mood and having fun together. I went to the kitchen to get something, and the moment I stepped in, the light came on all by itself. I stepped backward and out of the kitchen just as it happened, and the light went out. I stepped back across the threshold, and the kitchen light came on all by itself again. By this time everybody there had noticed what was going on, and they started egging me on to keep it up. So there I was, stepping in and out of the kitchen, and every time I stepped in that light would come on, and every time I stepped out it shut off. We had so much fun with it that eventually everybody started singing a wild tune and I was dancing at the doorway, slipping my toes in and making the light come on, then tapping my toes back out to make the light go out. We made a regular game out of it, and it kept up as long as we kept singing and dancing. There were eight or ten of us there, and everyone was really getting in to it. Eventually, we just got tired and stopped, and then the light stopped playing with us. We thought that one was pretty cool.

Pretty cool, indeed. With ghosts this friendly, it would appear the next step would be to attempt more intimate contact, if possible. That's exactly what this raucous group of thespians settled in to do. At an agreed-upon time they convened in the basement of the Beckwith to make contact with the spirits through the use of a Ouija board. Big mistake.

"In March of 2002," says Lacy,

a group of us got together to try to find out through the Ouija board who these people were who were haunting our beloved theater. We gathered down in the basement, turned off all the lights, and lit a few candles. We then positioned our chairs around a table, and started using the board.

At first, the mood was sort of fun, but with the lights out and candles casting shadows against walls you know harbor ghosts, attitudes change real quick. "I have to admit," she says,

that we weren't one minute into the session when I plain chickened out. Pretty soon, everyone else is starting to feel really spooked out about it, and the feeling was they needed to back off. The room started to feel overbearing, and we could sense something sinister all around us. One of the girls with us was only about fourteen years old. She was really scared and she started to cry. Everyone was at that point of fear where you're almost afraid to move. Anyway, there we were, all around this table with nothing but candles lighting up the darkened room, and when I looked across the table at that young girl, whose name I really don't want to give out, I saw a shadowy figure start to emerge from the wall behind her. The room was really dark, so this image was a few shades lighter, sort of a medium grey. Everybody else at the table saw it, and we just stared in disbelief. But since it was behind her, she couldn't see it, and am I ever thankful for that. But she could sense something wasn't right because by now she was almost hysterical. All we could do was sit there and watch as this shadowy entity emerged from the wall and slowly moved toward her. It came up behind her and stood over her from behind. She's crying and sobbing from fear, and we're trying not to show how scared we are. Then it backed away and sunk back into the wall behind her. That's when we turned on the lights, blew out the candles, and went home. We were too scared to even talk about it right away. I don't think I'll ever play around with one of those boards again!

I am amazed at how many people admit to me they engage in Ouija board use. As a rule, I avoid it altogether, if for no other reason than what the power of suggestion can do while fooling around with one. And I have been admonished time and again by kind folk who consider themselves psychic to advise those I meet with to avoid its use, even going so far as insisting that they remove the boards from their homes. For the gang at the Beckwith, it seems they learned the hard way down in that darkened basement.

Although the experience with the Ouija board proved to toss a wet blanket on their hopes of learning more about their ghosts, the folks at the Beckwith are still at ease with the spirits in their theater. And they still encounter new ghosts as time goes by. "Just a few weeks ago," says Lacy,

I was in the building doing some painting. When you're the executive director, it's not all privilege and position. There's a lot of work to do, and we all chip in together to get it done. Well, I was getting ready to paint, and I was up on the main floor, in the area where the patrons would pass through to go into the auditorium. I wanted a particular can of paint and thought it was probably downstairs. For some reason, I was instantly drawn to the stairwell off to the side of the stage, clear over on the other side of the auditorium, and knew I had to look down there. I walked over to the stairwell, not certain what I would encounter. The only light in the area was the exit light, and it was glowing red, casting its light down that stairwell. When I looked down into the stairwell, I could see a person hovering down at the bottom. It looked like a young girl, a teenager, and she was hunched down like someone would do if they didn't want to be seen. I couldn't believe what I was seeing, and I ran to get someone, to see if they could see it, too. When we came back to the stairwell, she was still there, hunkered down in the corner with a blanket around her head. It was as scary as scary can get—the light casting an eerie light red glow down the stairway, the girl huddled down on the floor down there, and us standing in the dark watching her. Then she slowly raised her head and looked straight at us, with this really pitiful expression on her face. We left in a hurry. Later, we used the Ouija board and asked it who this girl was. It told us she was an orphan who lived a century ago and who had no place to go. This was before the bad incident we had with the Ouija board down in the basement.

The impression Lacy and her girlfriend had was that this so-called orphan girl was there all the time. That was confirmed just a short while later when another cast member at the theater had an odd brush with her. "A new girl, Jennie, came to play a part in one of our productions", says Lacy.

She was sensitive to things paranormal and just a real sensitive person by personality. One day, she came to me and asked me if I had any fear of that back stairwell. She told me that for some reason she was terrified of the thought of having to use it. She went on to say that whenever she thought of the stairwell, or even looked at it, she would get the strong impression of a young girl hiding down there. I could tell she wasn't making this up, because me and my girlfriend hadn't said anything to anyone about what we had seen. Besides, Jennie was crying as she told me all this; she was that shaken. After she composed herself, she admitted to me that she had gone over to use the stairway once and was stopped short at the top when she looked down and saw a young girl crouched at the bottom with a blanket wrapped around her. Poor Jennie was terrified.

Author's Note: One of the results of my extended interview with Lacy was an invitation to spend the night investigating the historic Beckwith Theatre. I told her I would love to spend the night there and that I would make arrangements—which at the time of this writing are incomplete—to do so. She told me of how on several occasions others have tried to spend the night there, but none of them quite made it, all of them opting for the security of more comfortable digs. I assured her I have yet to be run out of any place by a ghost and that I doubted the Beckwith spirits could convince me to cut a hasty retreat. So, in the near future I plan to take Lacy up on her kind invitation.

6

The Ghostly Caregiver

Location of Haunting: The old, historic St. Francis Hospital building in the city of Escanaba on Michigan's Upper Peninsula.

Period of Haunting: This haunting seems to cover several decades—or at least its legend does. Some folks speak of having encountered the ghost of this edifice as far back as the 1950s, while others report more recent experiences. They all insist the ghost is quite nice, bringing a word of comfort to folks in despair.

Date of Investigation: Fall of 2001.

Description of Location: Sometime in the 1980s the Sisters of St. Francis dedicated a new hospital complex on the north side of Escanaba, leaving behind its previous, antiquated facility downtown. The haunting herein applies to the old hospital, a four-story structure of dark brick, dating back to the early part of the twentieth century. The architecture is rather stoic, with the appropriate Catholic flourishes. Although close to downtown Escanaba, it sits in a residential section of the city, just to the west of Ludington Street.

Escanaba is located on the extreme northern tip of Lake Michigan. It is a well-maintained community, relying heavily upon tourism for its income. For many, it is the epitome of "Yooper" living, offering great hunting and fishing in nearby forests, streams, and lakes. (By the way, a "Yooper" is any natural-born resident of the

U.P. or Upper Peninsula.) There is some light industry in the area, and many folks make their living in small businesses or as laborers in the lumbering trade. Mead Paper Company is the major employer in the area, and any local hired by them is considered to have found favor with the gods. St. Francis Hospital is also considered a major employer of Delta County, home to "Esky," as the residents refer to their city. Recently, Jeff Daniels, the actor from Chelsea, Michigan, filmed his original movie, *Escanaba in da Moonlight*, on location there, using, as he often and generously does, many of the local residents as extras.

To get to the old hospital, take US-2 west from the Mackinac Bridge. You'll travel about two and a half hours, passing through Manistique on the way. Upon entering Escanaba, look for the mall on your right, then go to the next stoplight, which is Ludington Street. Turn left and head down the main business district. You'll find 14th Street at a stoplight downtown. Turn right; the old St. Francis Hospital is just a couple blocks away.

Since ghosthunting and traveling great distances work up the appetite, a great meal is in order. When you're ready to dine, go back out to US-2 and backtrack east out of the city. Where Little Bay de Noc splashes up against the highway, look to your left and see the Log Cabin Supper Club nestled within the tall pines atop a small rise. Take a seat by the windows and dine with a terrific view of the bay. This is a fine eatery where the waitstaff doesn't need to ask you if everything is all right; they already know it is. Enjoy the whitefish, or opt for one of their great steaks. Sip a glass of white wine and relax; you truly are in a gorgeous part of Michigan. Afterwards, book a room at the Terrace Motor Inn, also right on the bay and just down the road from the Log Cabin. In the morning, shoot east into Gladstone for breakfast at the Dew Drop Inn. It's popular with the locals, and seating can sometimes be tough to find, but it's more than worth the trip. The portions are huge, and the inn is famous for its cinnamon rolls—large enough for two and so sweet they offer insulin shots if you down the whole thing in one sitting. When finished, drive on back to Escanaba and follow Ludington Street back through town until it dead ends at Ludington Park, right on the Bay. Digest your food to the views of rippling waters, ore boats, and pleasant folks like you just relaxing away the day.

The Haunt Meter: * *
Not frightening, but quite fascinating.

Lana Buckner (not her real name) was distraught. Her five-year-old daughter, Lucy, had been struck by a car earlier that evening while riding her bicycle. Now Lana was sitting in the consultation room with the surgeon as he explained the surgical procedure they were about to perform on little Lucy. It appears her spleen was ruptured, and there were most likely other internal injuries

Although Lana was in the company of family and friends who had all flocked to the hospital upon hearing the tragic news, her husband, Garrett, was out of town on business. "I managed to track him down," says Lana, "and he said he would catch the earliest flight he could find, but that he most certainly couldn't get there before morning. That was the tough part for me, because I needed him to be with me right then, I was so scared."

As the surgery progressed, family members and friends continued to filter in and out of the waiting room. Lana's pastor visited, offering comfort and prayer, and her mother arrived from Steven's Point, Wisconsin. Still, as any parent could tell you at a time like this, no amount of comfort can assuage the fear of losing a child, and no pain can match the agony of being a helpless parent in such a tenuous position.

By eleven that night, most of the support group had drifted back home, offering their kind thoughts as they departed. The hospital wing had grown silent, and the corridors were darkened by the shadows of night. By midnight, the surgery had gone into its fourth hour, and Lana was quickly approaching her breaking point. "All of a sudden," she says,

> I couldn't take it anymore. I had to get out of that waiting room. I wanted to go off alone somewhere, anywhere, and be by myself. I jumped up off the couch and told my mom I had to take a walk, that I was going down to the chapel. She said she'd go with me, but I told her I needed to be alone and that I'd be back in a few minutes. I told her if anyone gave her any news to come and get me right away.

Lana never made it to the chapel on another floor. She found a bench in one of the darkened hallways and slumped down into it, sobbing. "I have never felt so low," says Lana.

> For about ten minutes I couldn't stop shaking and crying. Then I composed myself as best I could and stood up to go back to the waiting room. As I stood there, I could hear the sound of someone coming down the hallway behind me. I glanced back and saw a black man coming my way, pushing a mop bucket. I figured he was the night janitor. He caught my eye and smiled this really warm, gentle smile. Somehow I knew he knew what I was going through. As he walked toward me, I could see he was wearing blue coveralls and that he was a large man, not fat, but very large and well built. He walked over and very lovingly put his arms around me. As he hugged me with those huge arms he said to me, "I'm here to tell you everything's going to be all right. Your little Lucy will be fine." Then he took his arms away and went back to his bucket. I thanked him and started back down to the family waiting room. I'd only gone a few steps when I turned around again, but he was gone. I couldn't see him anywhere, and I couldn't hear the sound of his mop bucket, which had been really squeaky at first. All of a sudden I realized I wasn't as frightened anymore. I had a calmness about me that said everything was going to be okay.

As it turned out, Lana's daughter Lucy survived the surgery and embarked on the road to recovery. During one of Lana's visits to her daughter, she recalled the incident with the janitor the night of the surgery. Wanting to thank him for his comfort, she asked about him at the nurse's station. They said they couldn't recall any janitor working that floor past 11 P.M. and referred her to the personnel department. Upon making inquiries there, Lana soon discovered there not only weren't any black janitors on staff, but there were no black employees at the hospital at all at that time. "It was the strangest thing that's ever happened to me," says Lana. "I know he was real, yet I believe he really wasn't. I like to think he was an angel, sent to give me hope when I was so torn up about Lucy."

It's possible Lana truly did encounter an angel. She certainly wouldn't be the first person to have such an encounter. Books and magazines are full of similar stories from all over the country. So why would I include this tale in my book about Michigan hauntings? To tell the truth, I wouldn't have except for the fact that Lana is not the only one to have encountered this comforting soul at St. Francis Hospital.

While visiting the Upper Peninsula to investigate two separate hauntings, I stopped off in Escanaba for lunch. As I am wont to do, I strike up conversations with waiters and waitresses about the journalistic nature of my visit. During this particular meal, the waitress, upon hearing of my escapades as a ghost afficionado, asked me if I'd ever heard of the ghost of old St. Francis Hospital. I feigned ignorance so as not to influence the tale she was about to relate, and opened my already attentive ears to the young woman I shall refer to as Tina. Here is her tale.

My father was in the hospital for cancer surgery, and it looked really serious. We were all afraid he wasn't going to make it. It was cancer of the stomach, and the doctors said it was pretty bad. My mom and all of us kids spent the day before the surgery with him in his room, but I think all we really did was make him more nervous and scared. I loved my dad a lot and couldn't stand even thinking about losing him.

Late in the evening, Dad said it was time for us to go home and get some rest. He's always been a really private person, and we all knew he really needed to be alone for a while. We all kissed him goodbye and tried to be upbeat, but there's no way he couldn't tell how scared we were. We led my mom out of the room, and told Dad we'd be back early enough in the morning to see him before they took him in to surgery.

When we got back to the hospital about 6 A.M., Dad was in a completely different mood. I mean, he was really okay now and didn't seem to be scared at all. When they came in to prep him we all had to leave except my mom, who stayed a while longer with him. We waited for her in the waiting room. When she finally came in, she seemed a little better, too. Then she told us why Dad was doing so good. He told her that after we had all left the night before, he couldn't sleep, which is pretty natural, I'd say. After a while, he said a man came into his room and stood in the doorway. At first he thought it was the janitor, but his room had been cleaned that afternoon. Then he said the man smiled really nice and friendly-like and told him he had a message for him. He told Dad that he was going to be all right, and that the operation was going to be a success. Then, according to Dad, the man just vanished.

After listening to Tina's tale, I couldn't resist asking if the man had any distinguishing features. She said, "No, I don't think so. The only thing Dad said about him was that he was really big, and that he was black." Bingo.

Could this have been an angel these distraught folks encountered in their moment of dire distress? Or could it be the spirit of someone who once worked at the hospital and is now long-deceased, yet still of a mind to give comfort to the hurting? I have no answers and will allow you the freedom to determine your own.

The Jackson Antique Mall.

7

Antique Ghosts

Location of Haunting: The Jackson Antique Mall is located at 201 N. Jackson Street in downtown Jackson, Michigan. It's an historic, somewhat narrow, two-story building on the corner of Jackson and Pearl Streets. Its location is only a couple of blocks away from another purportedly haunted historic building, the Michigan Theatre.

Period of Haunting: The present owners of the Jackson Antique Mall, Tim Bos and Bonnie Kresge, have operated their business at that location for the past ten years. They noticed ghostly activity immediately upon their arrival, so it is suspected that the structure has been haunted for several decades. At least one of the apparitions appears to date from the early third of the twentieth century.

Date of Investigation: Often, while engaged in autograph sessions at bookstores and libraries, people will regale me with tales of the macabre. They frequently are legendary stories that have grown larger than paranormal life and are more imaginary than historical. However, many of these leads serve as an introduction to what I consider a legitimate haunting. In the case of the Jackson Antique Mall, several persons at various times mentioned it as a great spot to spot a ghost. I even received e-mail from a few persons about the building, and at least one self-proclaimed psychic assured me the place was indeed inhabited by at least one person long since deceased. With so many referrals pouring in, I decided to wander over to the place myself and check out the wares.

Pretending to be a customer, I perused the shelves and display units and, much to my delight, found a few items I couldn't live without. While laying out my cold hard cash, I casually mentioned to the two women behind the main counter that theirs was a charming old building. They agreed, and then I remarked how the place probably had a ghost or two. Without hesitation, and in matter-of-fact tones, they assured me that it certainly was haunted and that everyone who has ever worked there would substantiate their statement. After they spun a few personal tales of unsettling experiences, I announced who I was and my real purpose in patronizing their establishment of needful things. I was cordially invited to return to speak to the owners and did so within a few days. I was given the run of the place for as long as I wished, and then blessed with an interview.

My, how I do drone on. The issue was, "Date of Investigation," wasn't it? That's easy, it was April of 2002.

Description of Location: The Jackson Antique Mall is typical of many downtown business structures of decades past. It is comprised of its original building, erected sometime in the 1860s, probably around the time the Civil War came to its protracted end. The upstairs section of the original building went up sometime in the 1870s. In the same decade, a drive-through carriage shop and livery stable were attached to the rear of the building. Later, well into the twentieth century, still another structure was attached to the second structure, resulting in what is now a rambling, one-and-a-half to two-story edifice, depending on which part you're standing in.

The owners, Tim and Bonnie, have begun extensive renovations to the building, preparing it inch-by-inch for the needs of their growing antique business. Tim is doing much of the work himself, often staying late to finish his chores. He is currently finishing off an old storage area in the basement, turning it into another display room. After completion, he intends to begin renovating the attic directly above the original structure. That attic was once used as an opera house and—how shall we say it?—a free market enterprise for affectionate encounters. At the present time it is a large, empty, open area with original hardwood flooring and tall, narrow windows. At one time there had been an outside entrance to the upstairs area, but it is now torn away and boarded over.

As for the first attached structure, the drive-through livery, Tim assures me that underneath the concrete are the remains of straw bedding mixed with the remains of equestrian calling cards. He also assures me that on damp days the former purpose of the structure offers an odor that proves its past.

In short, it is a building of mixed histories, quite interesting to visit.

The Haunt Meter: * * *

If the scoring of The Haunt Meter was based upon frequency of activity, it would merit a top score of five stars. However, it is based upon a "fright factor" of sorts, so even though the ghosts cavort around the place regularly and loudly, they really don't frighten folks very much.

Eleanor Lewis and Pam Bush were on duty the first time I visited. The first incident they related concerned wooden children's blocks, the type with a different letter on each side. I recall having played with such blocks as a child, never knowing their future value would far exceed their original cost. At any rate, the store is divided up into sections, with each section leased for a period of time by an independent antique dealer. It seems one dealer contracted the right-hand rear corner area of the main floor's original building as a place for his stash of oldies but goodies. On a shelf in that corner the dealer had displayed those wooden alphabet blocks, always arranging them from A to Z (I'm told the dealer was a real neat-freak). Countless times, upon opening the store for the day, those blocks, which had been neatly arranged just before closing the previous night, would be in a total state of disarray. To the hired help opening the store, it appeared to be a sort of "hey, I want your attention" statement.

I should point out that everyone associated with the building has agreed to call the main spirit in their midst "Blanche." It was never really made clear to me why they settled on this name, except to say that at least one employee is quite sensitive to activity of a paranormal nature and insists the ghost is a female who was associated with the building in a professional manner not long after its construction, and that the name given by the sensitive employee to the spirit was Blanche. At any rate, it appears that Blanche is the one responsible for almost all the activity throughout the rambling structure and will often take time out from her daily activities to speak to those who utter her name.

One afternoon, a former employee named Nina was busy showing a customer some items on a shelf in one of the booths—in fact, the same booth where the antique wooden blocks used to reside. Next to them was a ladder propped up against the wall, used to retrieve various wares stored at some height. As they rummaged together, the ladder began to slowly pull away from the wall, threatening to fall backward and onto a glass display case. The patron stared wide-eyed at the seemingly self-propelled ladder. Nina simply said, "All right, Blanche, put it back!" whereupon the ladder halted its rearward descent and gently moved back into position against the wall. While Nina was nonplussed by the whole affair, the patron decided upon a hasty purchase and even speedier exit.

While this incident seems extraordinarily invasive on Blanche's part, she has been even more forthcoming with yet another customer. I believe it was Pam Bush, a soft-spoken woman who has worked at the mall for quite some time, who told an even more fascinating tale of Blanche butting into a prospective sale.

Near the entrance of the store are long, glass display counters. Inside those counters are various antique pieces of jewelry and several old pocket watches. A customer showed interest in an antique bracelet with an unusual clasp and asked to try it on for size. She was having difficulty securing the clasp with her one free hand and asked one of the salesclerks for help. Just as the salesperson approached her, the clasp suddenly swung forward on its own and snapped down into position. While it would appear Blanche was just trying to be helpful and ring up a commission of her own, it turned out to be "no sale" as the bug-eyed young woman slid into a panic, ripped off the bracelet, and sped out of the store.

This hasn't been the only sale that Blanche has interrupted. Early one morning, just after the store was opened for the day, a solitary customer was shopping inside the second section of the store on the main floor. She called a salesperson over for help with some glass-ware she was considering, and as the two chatted away, a glass bowl containing a glass fork and spoon flew off a countertop more than thirty feet away and landed on the floor. While the bowl remained intact, the fork and the spoon were both smashed. The customer asked, "Do you have a ghost in here?" to which the salesperson responded with an innocent and honest, "Yes." That seemed to satisfy the customer, who simply returned to her discussion about the glassware she was interested in. Some folks can take it, some folks can't.

As if this isn't enough to make any employee's day

*Pam Bush, an employee who knows Blanche
well and first told me the ghost's story.*

interesting, another ghost makes himself known by
stomping on the upstairs floor. In fact, that's what they
call him, The Stomper. "There's been many times when
all of a sudden we'll hear what sounds like someone
stamping their feet as hard as they can on the floor
above us," says Pam.

> It's not at all like someone walking around in heavy
> boots, but more like someone angry who's trying to get
> our attention. The area up there is empty, and cus-
> tomers aren't allowed in, so we know it's not them. You
> never know when it's going to happen. All of a sudden
> you hear the stomping, and then it stops.

For my return visit to the Jackson Antique Mall, I
arranged ahead of time to meet with Bonnie and Tim.
Bonnie is a friendly, outgoing woman who is in love with
antiques and claims to have been so since her youth.
Tim shares her devotion to items of yore and is very
knowledgeable about his profession. In fact, he is a

professional appraiser, often helping attorneys value estates. Both are fascinating people to talk with and are willing to spend whatever time it takes to help you make an informed purchase. My conversation with them was interesting, although I had to follow Tim around quite a bit, as he is a slender bundle of energy.

It was Bonnie who first noticed that something was a bit out of the ordinary in their newly purchased building. Not long after setting up shop, she and Tim remained at the store after closing, arranging stock and making the old place a bit more appealing. "I had gone upstairs," says Bonnie, "and into what I call the opera room." (The opera room is the room directly above the original structure, but accessible only by going through the attic of the rear addition.)

> I put some things away in there, and then came out of the opera room and into the attached attic room. As I did, I saw a man standing over by the windows

The upstairs area of the Jackson Antique Mall, formerly a dance hall. The loud poundings emanate from here.

bordering Pearl Street. I sort of froze because I knew no one was supposed to be in the store. My first thought was to ask myself if I needed a weapon or something. Then I realized I could only see the man from the waist up, that the rest of him just wasn't there. It was about 5 or 6 P.M., so it wasn't dark up there, and I could see the man very clearly. He had a long mustache and was wearing a pea coat. He wasn't looking at me; in fact, I don't think he realized I was even there. He just stood there looking out the window, and then he just disappeared. My impression was that he was from the early 1900s.

Bonnie, by the way, is as frightened as the next person of an intruder, but not at all put off by a ghost. She tells me she grew up in a haunted house on the northwest side of Jackson and learned at an early age how to coexist peacefully with them.

Tim did not grow up with ghosts hanging around the house, but also is not the least bit put off by them. "When Blanche starts acting up around me," he says, "and I've got work to do, I yell at her to knock it off, and she lays off." Perhaps this is advice we can all use, especially those of us who don't know what to say or do when a spirit gets playful around us.

While it appears Blanche is the main entity of the establishment, and other spirits come and go, there seems to be more to this haunting than the shenanigans of the deceased. Early in their first year of residence, Tim and Bonnie were regularly spending their evenings engaged in restoration work. Very late one night, while Tim was on the main floor, Bonnie went upstairs to attend to some chores.

"I went upstairs," she says,

around 2 A.M. to do some work up there. As soon as I stepped off the staircase and into the room, I saw this huge green, glowing, swirling mass of light. It was at about the middle of the room, and it kept slowly moving around in a pulsating sort of way. I remember asking myself just what the hell was going on. This thing was huge! It was about eight feet wide and went from floor to ceiling, with all sorts of green colors glowing as it moved around and around and up toward the ceiling. It had a real lazy electric look to it. My first thought was that it would start a fire, and then I realized it wasn't hot. I figured it must be some lights from outside coming through the windows, so I wanted to check it out and see where it was coming from. The only way to look out the window was to walk past it, which didn't bother me any. I went over to the window, but the night was perfectly dark and there was no way it could have come from outside. At that moment I thought I'd better go get Tim, and by the time I walked past it again, it had grown even bigger and had a bit of a humming noise to it. This time, I had to brush up against it as I went by, and when I did, the hair on my arm started to tingle. When I got to the other side of the room, I looked back at it. Then it started to get lazier and slow danced downward, getting lighter green as it went. Then it seemed to disappear down into the

Upstairs display area at the Jackson Park Antique Mall.
Blanche is often seen looking out the window on the far left.

floor and was gone. I ran down to get Tim and tell him about it, but when he went back up there with me, there was no sign of it.

The strange activities associated with the antique store may not be linked only to the building itself. There is a theory that spirits often are connected with personal belongings they were once strongly attached to in life. If that's the case, then antique emporiums everywhere must be absolute havens of paranormal activity. Tim seems to have had at least one profound encounter with an entity strongly attached to a grandfather clock.

An elderly woman in the community was quite ill, and one of her children from Florida took her home to live with him so he could care for her. While in Michigan to make these arrangements, I appraised some items for the family. The old lady had a grandfather clock I was really attracted to, so I asked if I could buy it. They sold it to me, and I took it to my shop and put it on display.

Tim wasn't sure he wanted to part with the clock and he was concerned that many people would show interest in it. But as it turned out, after three weeks on display no one paid it any notice. In fact, they actually seemed to be repulsed by it for some reason.

"One night, about 2 A.M.," says Tim,

I suddenly woke up in a panic. For some reason I knew I had to get down to the store and get that clock. I drove on over and brought it back home. I put it in my living room and sat down and looked at it. I could just sense a strange attachment between it and me. Then I got up opened the door of the clock, set the time for 2:26 A.M., and swung the pendulum. Just as I did, a big rush of cold air gushed out of there and into the room. It swirled like a whirlwind all through the room. I just stood there in total amazement. I knew right away that this was the woman who had owned the clock; it was like I could sense her and almost see her there. Then it was gone.

If that's not enough to raise the hackles of any ghost afficionado, what follows should at least give them pause for reflection.

"About a month later," says Tim,

> the woman's son was up in Michigan again on business and I happened to run into him. I asked about his mother and he said she had passed away. I asked, "was it on a Wednesday?" and he said it was. Then I asked, "was it at 2:26 A.M.?" and the man said that, yeah, he had sat up with his mother until the end, and she died at 2:26 in the morning. Then he wanted to know how I knew these things, and when I told him the story, he was wide-eyed in amazement.

Floating ladders, swirling green masses, flying glassware, and ghostly figures showing up from time to time would be enough to qualify any home or place of business as haunted. And if this story constitutes a seven-course meal for any champion of the paranormal, then what follows is dessert.

"A man came in a couple of years ago from Georgia," says Tim.

> He dealt in antiques, and he had a beautiful antique bedroom set which dated back to the Civil War. He said he picked it up in Atlanta. It was cottage style, with a huge headboard sporting a hand-carved ship. Included was a night stand, a table, and three chairs. This sort of furniture was popular with gentlemen in the antebellum age, and the table and chairs would have been used for when the gentleman of the house would take his men-friends upstairs for a game of poker. Such activity would have been improper in the presence of ladies.

It appears this bedroom set, which also included a dresser, was damaged when Union General Sherman cut his sixty-mile-wide swath across Georgia, burning everything along the way.

"The set was in great condition," says Tim,

Tim Bos, co-owner of the Jackson Antique Mall, has experienced many unusual goings-on inside his establishment.

and was really quite valuable. But it did have a musty smell, and I could tell it came from smoke damage. There should have been an armoire and a fourth chair, but I figured they were probably lost in the fire. The history connected to the set was really fascinating. Anyway, I put the set on display in the second room of the shop, over near the back corner. It wasn't long before we figured there was something strange about it. Every time we'd walk toward it, the air would get colder and colder, until it was really cold right next to it. I found it very hard to go anywhere near it—it felt like there was some sort of entity attached to it, someone who didn't want anyone around it.

It wasn't long before the employees of the shop discovered the bedroom set gave them a good case of the willies too. In fact, so strong and so constant was the eerie coldness that Tim eventually began to amuse himself with a little mischievous game.

> For fun, Bonnie and I would send different employees into the room to turn off the lights at the end of the day. The lights are in the back corner of the room, and you had to pass right by the bedroom set to get to them. We'd watch them head that direction, and then turn off and try to get to the lights without going near that furniture. Usually, they'd just stop altogether, and ask someone else to switch off the lights.

The hired help weren't the only ones to be repulsed by that cursed set of furniture. Tim and Bonnie still laugh about how they'd watch customers as they wandered through the store, looking first at one thing and then at another. "Then," says Tim,

> they'd innocently start wandering in the direction of that furniture and, almost without fail, unconsciously curve away and avoid it altogether. We couldn't believe how often that happened. We got a lot of chuckles out of it.

While they may have gotten a few laughs out of that furniture, they weren't getting any bites on it. "No one—and I mean no one—showed any interest in it," says Tim.

> It was an absolutely fabulous set, but people avoided it, never even asked about it. You didn't have to be a believer in ghosts or spirits or hauntings, just watching people react to that set made you a believer.

Eventually, Tim decided to check out that bedroom set for himself. "I decided one day I was going to try it out," says Tim.

> The bedframe was already set up on display, so I brought over a mattress and set in on the frame. Then I lay down on the mattress to see what it was like. As

soon as I did, I got this intense swirling, spinning sensation, and I got really dizzy, like the room was spinning. I thought I would get sick to my stomach, so I got off right away. From that point on, I just left it alone.

One can only speculate who, or what, was haunting that period set. Was it the ghost of the original gentleman owner? Or did someone else die in the fire that consumed some of the other pieces, only to find themselves stuck in time with the furniture? Tim has no idea what the haunting is all about, but he and Bonnie do know it cost them some real cash. "That set should have sold for around $4,000," says Bonnie, "and we had it for so long that we eventually had to let it go for less than half that much."

A sideline to this tale involves an unsolicited letter I received from a woman named Suki Wheeler. Suki has never worked at the antique store, but has visited it quite often, both as customer and interested psychic. In her letter, Suki says she has seen Blanche, the main ghost of the building. She says she was passing by one time, on her way to visit friends, and saw Blanche standing in the upstairs window overlooking Pearl Street. She was wearing a white blouse and didn't wave back when Suki attempted to exchange that particular nicety. According to Suki, Blanche was a madam and ran a brothel in the upstairs portion of the antique store. She also believes Blanche met a violent death inside the building and remains there to watch over it, much as she did when she operated her business.

Suki senses that other people can see Blanche on occasion, but that mostly they just sense her or experience her playful pranks. So clearly does Suki "see" Blanche, that she drew a couple pictures of her and sent them along to me. She appears to be a beautiful young woman with large, dark eyes and shoulder-length brown hair.

*A drawing of Blanche, the ghost, by Suki Wheeler, a
psychic who often visits the Jackson Park Antique Mall.*

During my numerous visits to the Jackson Antique Mall, I always felt very comfortable. Everyone there insists Blanche is not malevolent and I am fully inclined to believe them.

When I finished my last visit at the old antique store, I asked Tim if he ever once felt frightened by the place. His response was endearing. "Not at all," he said. "In fact, I love the place. Every time I walk past it, I pat it and tell it I love it. And if there are ghosts in there, they're welcome to stay."

The Jackson Antique Mall is a great place to shop. I have discovered their prices to be reasonable and the help most courteous. Undoubtedly, some readers will be racing over there to check the place out for themselves. If you're one of them, you'll be made welcome, but remember that it's a place of business and to give the place, and the people, the respect they're due.

8

Added Attraction

Location of Haunting: The Michigan Theatre is located at 124 N. Mechanic, in downtown Jackson, Michigan.

Period of Haunting: Exactly how long the supposed haunting has been taking place is difficult to say. At least one of the two accounts related here is quite recent and if, as the story relates, children are most sensitive to the spirit(s) in this ornate edifice, then perhaps more than one child has gotten an extra prize with their popcorn.

Date of Investigation: Twice during the spring and summer of 2001, with the main lead supplied to me in December of 2000.

Description of Location: The Michigan Theatre is a beautiful movie house reminiscent of the movie palaces of bygone eras. With its gilded chandeliers and sweeping balcony, it is a grand reminder of how impressive entertainment houses were when our parents and grandparents plopped down their nickels to watch the latest flick. It was the place to see a film as far back as the 1920s and was the dominant theater in Jackson until the early 1970s. In a day when movie theaters now boast twenty screens, each not much larger than your living room wall, the Michigan Theatre overwhelms modern patrons with one grand silver screen rising from floor to ceiling displaying its tinsel-town images before hundreds of seats. So thrilled with its grandeur was actor Jeff Daniels, that he chose to premier his new movie, *Super Sucker*, within its gilded walls. This is one of the few

The haunted Michigan Theatre in downtown Jackson, Michigan.

theaters in existence that looks, feels, and even smells like an old-time movie house.

To experience a movie, or for that matter a live performance, travel I-94 to the US-127 exit and go south to Michigan Avenue. Follow Michigan Avenue west until you reach the old train depot (still in operation) on your left. Remain on course and the road will become a four-lane, one-way thoroughfare. When it does, look off to your left and you'll see the grand old marquis piercing the night skies. Turn left on Mechanic and you're there. Should you wish to enjoy an intimate dinner beforehand, backtrack east on Michigan Avenue and go under the US-127 overpass a few blocks to a restaurant named Tom's. It's been around for decades and still boasts some of the finest food and drink anywhere in the area—one of those places where the waitstaff actually understands the menu and how to serve a customer with a little class.

The Haunt Meter: * * *

Judging from the restoration still in progress, the Michigan Theatre likely looked haunted the day it opened its doors.

Katie Stone is well acquainted with the Michigan Theatre, having patronized the establishment quite often as a child. "When I was a kid," she relates, "the big deal with that place was to throw popcorn up in the air to watch the bats swoop down from the balcony. I still don't like the balcony and won't go up there!"

Katie continues the tradition of class moviegoing by treating her children to films and live performances whenever she can. From the start, her kids realized something was just not right, complaining of a strange chill in the air from time to time. She says, "they have decided that it is uncomfortably cold in there sometimes and have begun to ask me why. I've told them I really don't know why, but I take a blanket with us now just in case."

The most profound experience Katie tells concerns her son Jake. When he was about three years old, Katie took Jake to the Michigan Theatre to see a special children's movie. As Katie tells it . . .

> We were sitting to the left of the middle section, about ten rows from the screen. The movie was playing, and Jake was chattering away. I nudged him to get his attention and he looked at me. I pointed to the screen and he quieted down. A few minutes later, he was chattering away again, and I leaned over and explained to him that it was rude to talk while the movie was playing. That's when Jake said, "But HE'S talking to ME!" Not seeing anyone in the direction he was looking, I said, "Who?" Jake said, "That man right over there!" Still unable to see anyone, I said, "What's he wearing?" Jake went on to describe a man in a dress shirt, vest, and top hat. He even asked me if I could see the shiny chain on his vest. I figured it was a pocket watch and, at that moment, also determined it must be a ghost he was seeing. Finally, I asked Jake, "Well, what does he want?" Jake started to get up from his seat while saying the man wanted him to come over there. I stopped him with my arm, firmly telling him, "You tell that man that your mother said you are not going anywhere! Now you stay here and watch the movie!" Jake looked in the direction of whoever or whatever was there and just shook his head. He glanced over now and then during the rest of the movie and finally told me the man had left.

Katie goes on to say that she has been in that theater a thousand times and had never once experienced anything more frightening than the dive-bombing bats, although, "Sometimes it just suddenly gets really cold in some places." This kind of story sort of makes you wonder if some ghosts prey upon the innocence of young children. At any rate, Katie seemed none too happy about her son's encounter with the top-hatted apparition in the high-class duds.

Katie is not the only one to offer me a story or two about the grand and glorious Michigan Theatre. Several folks have come forward with their own tales, such as the one Brenda B. and her husband Ken told.

Not willing to offer their full names for fear of the ridicule of neighbors and friends, I agreed to hear their story and keep them under the umbrella of a low profile. Their story could easily elicit such admonitions.

We went out for dinner and a movie—this was back in the early 1970s—and the movie was *The Godfather.* It was really popular then and Ken was dying to see it. As for me, I didn't think it was much of a dinner-and-a-date movie, but I agreed. The place was really packed, and we either had to sit real close to the screen or go up to the balcony. Well, I didn't like the balcony because it's really steep up there, and if you miss your step there's not much to keep you from falling over the railing and landing on top of someone down below. Anyway, it made me dizzy just being up there.

At this point in time I can't recall if it had an official intermission, but the movie was long. About three-quarters of the way through the movie I decided I couldn't hold the pop any longer and asked Ken if he'd take me to the restroom. We went up the stairs to the balcony level because the restrooms were larger there and we figured there would be less waiting. As I started to enter the ladies' room, I instinctively stepped aside for an elderly woman who was coming out. Just as she passed me I thought, that's not right," and turned around to take a better look. She was walking away from the ladies' room and over to where the stairs went up again to the balcony seating. She was all dressed in clothes from the 1920s or '30s, the long dress and funny feathered cap. She really seemed out of place, but I figured maybe she had dressed that way for the movie, which I guess takes place around that time period, although no one else was wearing period costume. Anyway, when I finished in the ladies' room, Ken was waiting for me outside. I remarked to him about the strange old woman in the old-style clothing, and he told me she was stranger than I thought. He said he had seen her come out of the ladies' room and walk over to the balcony entrance. Then she had just stood there for a few moments and sort of glided up the stairs. I guess he was struck by how strange she was too, because he went up another staircase to the balcony to check her out, but when he got there she was gone. It really weirded us out at the time.

The Michigan Theatre is now under the tender loving care of a privately-owned consortium dedicated to its refurbishment. They have begun the painstaking task of raising the cash needed to restore the wonderful old building, and work continues.

I have a bit of a connection to this story, as I can remember standing in long lines there more than once to catch Charlton Heston matching Biblical plagues with Yul Brynner in the re-release of Cecil B. DeMille's *The Ten Commandments* back in the 1960s. It was also where I first viewed the dashing elegance of Clark Gable as he strode two steps at a time upward toward the boudoir with Vivien Leigh in his arms in Margaret Mitchell's *Gone With the Wind*—although I'm glad to say I wasn't old enough to catch the original release. And just like Brenda and Ken, I caught *The Godfather* in that very same theater. (I wonder if it was the same night as their ghostly encounter?) And if that's not enough, I recently took my family for one of their wonderful live performances and, sure enough, the bats appeared as an added attraction.

If you have the inkling to do so, go on over to the Michigan Theatre. Both you and the caretakers will benefit from the experience. They will receive your price of admission, which helps with their restoration efforts, and you may bear witness to a ghost or two, in addition to one of the fine films they so lovingly offer.

9

Hired Help

Location of Haunting: A farmhouse, like any other farmhouse, in the sprawling farmlands around Leslie, Michigan, about twenty minutes south of Lansing.

Period of Haunting: According to the respondents, this haunting has taken place sporadically over the last decade or so. Some of the appearances of this "farmer ghost" and his woman companion have been quite recent.

Date of Investigation: I first heard about this haunting during a 2001 book signing at the WaldenBooks inside the Westwood Mall in Jackson, Michigan. Arrangements were made to meet with the owners of the home, and hence the details poured forth.

Description of Location: Leslie is a small town in south central Michigan, about twelve miles north of Jackson. Though not a large community by any stretch of the imagination, it is a proud community. The citizens have built a new, magnificent high school facility, and the community is quick to support their Blackhawks in all their athletic endeavors. Leslie is about a twenty-mile drive from Lansing and East Lansing, two distinctly different cities, and therefore supportive also of the Michigan State Spartans. To get to Leslie, travel I-94 to US-127 and head north. Drive about twelve miles and you'll see the Leslie exit. Don't miss it, as it's the only immediate exit off the freeway and into town.

The Haunt Meter: * * *

For a small, rural community, Leslie could easily become notorious as one of the more haunted places in Michigan. Judging from the contacts I've had and leads I've been given, just about every other farm outside of town has its own resident ghost, as do half the houses inside the city limits as well. Some of the leads directed my way sounded promising, but, alas, didn't pan out for one reason or another. Other leads fell flat when I discovered the folks involved had moved away, leaving no forwarding address. I therefore decided to narrow things down to a single haunt.

Not far from the outskirts of Leslie sits a typical farmhouse, surrounded by barns and outbuildings and fields of whatever they decide to plant during any given year. Inside that house dwell the Clovers (not their real name): father, mother, three kids, and at least two somewhat playful, if not annoying, ghosts.

Clarence Clover (hey, I had to come up with *some* name) and wife Bernice have farmed all their lives. They've lived at peace with their neighbors and their house for decades. That's why they're a bit mystified at the sporadic hijinks that have begun within the last ten years or so. They have no idea why it began when it did, or who it is who's haunting their previous place of residence.

"The first time I noticed something odd," says Clarence,

> I was heading home from having gone to the bank. I pulled in the driveway, and I saw someone standing off in the barn, just inside the door. I had a fellow coming out to buy some bales of straw from me, but that wasn't supposed to be until later. I figured maybe the guy showed up early, so I headed on over there. When I got there, there wasn't anybody there at all. I went back to the house and asked Bernice if the guy had shown up yet, and she said he hadn't, so I chalked it

up to just being a little tired and let it go at that.

Nothing further was mentioned about what Clarence thought he saw, until one of his friends stopped by a few weeks later for coffee and the requisite farm talk. "This buddy of mine," says Clarence,

> came over for coffee one morning, and when he got out of his pickup I saw him stop for second or two and look over to the barn. Then he came in and asked me who it was that was in the barn. I told him no one was there that I knew of, and he said he saw a man standing just outside the barn door. I asked what he looked like, and he said it was a man who looked to be in his sixties, wearing bib overalls and a baseball cap. He didn't think anything of it, just thought I had somebody over to the house. That's when I told him I saw the same doggone guy once myself.

Whoever the ghost of the barn is, he seems harmless enough. Two of the kids have seen him, and even the family dog has wagged a tail and offered a bark or two in the direction of the ghost. While he does stand at watch over the family members as they go about their business, he shows no overt interaction with them.

"A couple years back," says Bernice,

> the kids got off the school bus and were walking up the drive. It was winter, so they were in a hurry to get inside. The two oldest said that as they got near the house, they saw a man standing near the barn, over by the fence. When I asked what he looked like they described the same man my husband and our friend saw. This made me a little nervous because now the kids were seeing this man and we hadn't said a word about him to them. I made up some excuse for going outside and I went over there, but there was no sign of him anywhere; it snowed that day, so there would have been tracks somewhere, but there wasn't.

The nearest Clarence and Bernice could tell, the man in question was a farmer. He was in his sixties and, though he wore a baseball cap, you could still make out a shock of gray hair above each ear. He appeared to be a stocky, well-built man with a pleasant face. No one in the family seemed to be afraid of him or of going out to the barn. They were just baffled about who he could be. It wasn't long, though, before they found themselves a bit more baffled, as yet another spirit floated its way into their lives and their home.

It appears the ghost who hangs around their barn, whom they've affectionately dubbed "Heck" (short for, *Who the heck is that?*) has a lady friend. Bernice was first to encounter this woman. "It was in October of 2000," she says.

> I had a couple pies in the oven for supper and went outside to get the mail. As soon as I closed the front door, I heard the lock snap shut and I knew I'd locked myself out of the house. I tried the door anyway and I couldn't get in. I started down the porch when I heard the lock snap again, and I looked back and the door was swinging open. I ran up the steps and into the living room just in time to catch a glimpse of a woman going upstairs. I was too scared to go up there, so I went to the kitchen. That's when things really got strange for me. My pies were now out of the oven and sitting on the counter next to the stove. That's when I *knew* I wasn't going upstairs for love nor money. I just stayed right there in the kitchen until the kids got home.

Bernice related the events of her day to her husband, and he assured her that if there was a ghost in the house, it must be a helpful one. Helpful or not, Bernice would just as soon handle the household chores herself. "I don't mind too much a ghost staying out by the barn, but I don't much care for one in my house, especially when I'm alone," says she. I suppose most folks feel the same.

This was not a singular encounter. A few weeks after the door and pie incident, the kids got a taste of this lady-ghost for themselves. The kids' bathroom is up-

*The stairway in a farmhouse near Leslie, Michigan, where
a ghostly woman is often seen by family members.*

stairs, between the bedrooms. Apparently, the youngest
of the clan was drawing water for a bath and left the tap
on while he went back to his room. The oldest child
could hear the water running and running and began to
holler for her little brother to go shut it off. Feeling
ignored, her anger rose and she began to holler even
louder for her brother to get into the bathroom and shut
off the water before it overflowed. Still receiving no
response, she stomped out of her room, past the bathroom where the water was gushing forth and into little
brother's bedroom, where she began to berate him for
being a jerk. Just then, they heard the water being shut
off, and they assumed mom had come to junior's rescue.
As big sis headed back to her room, she glanced inside
the bathroom only to see an empty room. Then, out of
the corner of her eye, she saw the blurry image of a
woman descending the staircase. All she caught was a
fleeting glimpse, but she knew it wasn't her mother.

The dutiful daughter reported the strange event to her mother, who assured her daughter she wasn't going crazy, that she had also encountered this lady. After comparing notes, they determined the woman to be in her late fifties or early sixties, with dark hair and a blue housedress. They agreed they most likely had nothing to fear from her, but also entered into a pact not to tell the other children.

The best the Clovers can figure is that the man in the barn and the woman in the house are linked together, and are probably husband and wife. But why they are there is a total mystery to them. They don't look like anyone they knew and certainly don't resemble any deceased relatives. It seems obvious they mean no harm and that they were once associated with a farm, but why would they show up at this farm? No one has any answers here, and the ghosts aren't talking.

10

The Ghost Who
Protects Her Domain

Location of Haunting: A single-family residence, tucked away within a meticulously manicured subdivision in Livonia, Michigan. The owners were determined not to let their address be included in this narrative. Just trying to live with their ghost is aggravation enough. They don't need any ghosthunters, regardless of how sincere, making their lives any more uncomfortable. The most I can say here is that this house is but a stone's throw from St. Mary's Hospital.

Period of Haunting: The haunting in question began in the early 1970s and continues, to a lesser extent, to this very day.

Date of Investigation: Reluctant to give an interview, these homeowners first contacted me by e-mail, congratulating me on the success of my first book. They read the book and found it credible (much to my delight), but when prodded to share the rather macabre experiences mentioned within their e-mail message, they were reluctant to elaborate. After a bit of back-and-forth electronic niceties, they finally felt me trustworthy enough to invite me to their home. That meeting, which ultimately led to this chapter, took place in the summer of 2001.

Description of Location: If appearances have anything to do with whether or not a home is prone to ghostly manifestations, then this abode ought to be pure as the driven snow, which is pretty pure considering the amount of snow this part of Michigan receives. But ghosts seem to be above appearances, inhabiting pristine suburban locales as readily as they haunt the stereotypical ramshackle dwellings of our vivid imaginations. Livonia is a rather upper-crust suburb of Detroit, offering just about every amenity a suburbanite could covet. If you, dear reader, find yourself in the area, drop by Laurel Park Mall for some upscale shopping or to catch a movie at its cavernous new multiplex.

The Haunt Meter: * * * *

Karla and Tom McKenzie (certainly not their real names) first encountered the spirit within their halls not long after moving into their home in the early 1990s. Both Karla and Tom have mid-management level positions in one of the several corporations with satellite offices in the area and purchased the house because of its convenient location to their respective places of employment.

Having set up housekeeping in the short frigid days of winter, Karla was more than a little pleased when spring brought forth its friendly sunshine and warmth. "I had been to Meijer's," says Karla,

> to pick up some wisteria for the garden I was putting in out back. Tom was out golfing and I was alone at the house. I took the plants out of the van and placed them in a wagon in the back yard. Tom had rototilled the garden area for me, but I had forgotten to get the fertilizer out of the house. So, I went in the house through the back door, got the fertilizer from the utility room, and went back out to the garden and started planting and fertilizing the wisteria. After a while I wanted a drink of water, so I walked back to the house. When I got to the back door, it was locked. Now, I couldn't recall having locked it, but I figured I could have, and since I always kept my keys on my person, I unlocked the door and went inside. That's when I first noticed something odd.

That "something odd" Karla noticed was a foul stench in the air. It seemed to permeate the kitchen and, as she tells it, smelled much like old, rotted meat.

"The smell was so bad," she says,

> that I couldn't even drink my water. So I set my glass down and started to look around in the kitchen—under the sink and in the trash bin—but I couldn't find anything spoiled. Then all of a sudden it was gone. Just like that. One second it's there and the next it's gone. I drank my water and went back outside to finish up the wisteria. Then, when I was all done, I headed back to the house, and the back door was locked again. I really didn't think it was much more than my own stupidity at locking the door twice, and I just let myself in. Little did I know it was just the start.

As it turns out, Karla's troubles with the back door was just a preview of coming attractions. And those attractions were less than welcomed.

"About a week after the first back door incident," recalls Karla,

> I ran out to the garage to get something out of my car. It was raining out, so I dashed out the door, grabbed what I needed, and dashed back to the house. When I got there the dang door was locked again. Now this time I know I didn't lock it. I was home alone and this time my keys were in my purse in the kitchen. There wasn't anything I could do, so I opened the big garage door, unfolded a chaise lounge, and lay down on it. I remember thinking how much I hoped the neighbors wouldn't see me all stretched out on a chaise lounge in my garage while the rain pounded down outside, but what else could I really do?

As luck would have it, Karla's moment of respite inside her garage was not without entertainment.

"I was sort of mad," she says,

> about being locked out of the house, but I knew there was no way I had locked that door. So I sat there watching the house. Pretty soon, I saw a dark figure of

a man pass by the kitchen window. Now this was at about 4 P.M. during the spring, and it's really light out. Anyone walking through the kitchen would have been easy to see, but this guy was like a solid shadow, and he had form. It only lasted a couple of seconds, but I knew I had really seen this guy. I sat up all in absolute disbelief staring at the house, wondering what in the world was going on. Not too awfully long after that, about the time I had calmed down a bit, he walked past again.

The finale to that afternoon's encounter was relayed to me in a state of mild embarrassment on Karla's part. She told me she ran to the neighbors' house, although she really didn't know them very well, and stood in the rain, knocking on their door. After a harried introduction and a couple of raised eyebrows, she was allowed to use the telephone.

"I still wonder what the neighbors thought of this kook standing in their living room, soaking wet, making hysterical phone calls," says Karla.

I phoned the police, and then I called Tom at work and told him to come straight home, that I saw someone in the kitchen. Well, I waited at the neighbors' house until two police cars pulled in the drive, and I called them over to the neighbors' house to tell them what I saw. They immediately went over and started looking through the windows and checking the doors, and about that time Tom got home. We went over and Tom unlocked the doors for the policemen, and they had us wait outside until they had checked the house out. I knew they wouldn't find anybody, and they didn't. But I also knew that something had been in my house.

Tom, for his part, really didn't doubt Karla's story. "She's not the crazy type," says Tom.

She's one of the most levelheaded women I know. I mean, she's an engineer, and engineers are the most logical, prove-it-to-me types in the world. That's why I knew she had seen something.

(As one who documents ghostly tales, I am intrigued with how often creative, artistic types encounter ghosts, and how the sequential-thinking, syllogistic types almost never run into a spook. That's why I found Karla's spectral testimony so fascinating. Or maybe this ghost just likes engineers.)

Even if Tom did have some reservations about his wife's sanity, he soon had proof for himself that something was amiss in the old homestead.

"It was a gorgeous Saturday morning," he says,

and we were going to go to Wampler's Lake with some friends of ours who have a pontoon. Karla was packing some things to take along with us, and I ran out to the garage to get my skis and life jackets from storage up in the attic. I put those things in the car and went back to the house to get the other stuff I needed to pack. When I got to the back door, it was locked. Now, since Karla had her experiences with the door I had checked it out several times to make sure you couldn't inadvertently lock yourself out. But it was locked. So, I knocked really loud but Karla never came. I knocked even harder, but still no Karla. I glanced around the yard a second or two to see if any neighbors were watching me pounding on the door to get into my own house, and when I turned back toward the door I saw this really hideous old man standing on the other side of the glass staring at me. I couldn't believe what I was seeing, his eyes were all sunk in and dark. He had stringy white hair that covered his ears, and he just look like death itself had been warmed up on the back burner. I was so shocked at the sight of him that I jumped back and actually thought I was going to throw up, and then he was gone.

Tom says he grabbed the doorknob at that point and it turned with ease, letting him back inside. He immediately called out to Karla, who was in the bedroom packing some clothes for the outing. She maintained she never heard Tom pounding on the door and never saw anything amiss. Needless to say, the events of the morning overshadowed the fun at the lake. After all, they did have to go home again.

Things were relatively peaceful for the next several weeks, and Tom and Karla nestled back into their daily routines, unencumbered by any rude apparitional activity. Just about the time their minds had nearly erased the memories of those strange moments, it all started afresh.

"We had gone to bed a little after midnight," says Karla,

and I was just rolling over to kiss Tom good-night. Just as I started to roll over, I saw this figure out of the corner of my eye. I real quick turned my head toward the door, and I could see this man standing just outside the doorway of the bedroom. Tom looked to see what I was looking at, and he saw the man, too. It wasn't real clear, but he was standing just in front of the hallway nightlight, so he was back-lit. He looked like an old man with white hair, and he just stood there, a little stooped over with his arms hanging limp at his sides. When he realized we were looking at him, a sort of sneering grin spread out over his face, and then he just turned and walked back down the hallway and into the living room and out of sight.

In response to this nocturnal interloping, Tom did what any red-blooded American would do at such a threatening moment—he froze.

"I have to admit," says Tom,

I felt no particular need to rush out to the living room and confront this guy. Eventually, I did go out there to check things out, but only because Karla was so ticked off that she started to get out of bed herself and go out there.

As I said earlier, Karla is a no-nonsense type of person, and perfectly willing to take on whoever, or whatever, was invading her privacy.

"I was livid," she says.

I mean, this is my home, and whatever this was had no business doing this to us. I knew right along it wasn't a real person, that it was some sort of ghost, and it sounds stupid that I thought I could confront it, but I trotted right out there to take it on. Tom was right behind me, but I think at that point I was more of a comfort to him than he was trying to be to me. When I got into the living room, of course he was nowhere to be found. We turned on all the lights and checked out the whole house, but naturally, all was quiet. I was still pretty mad, so I gave whatever it was a good cussing out—I heard somewhere that if you do that, they'll leave you alone. Then we went back to bed.

The ghostly old codger didn't leave them alone.

"Later in the summer," says Karla,

we had some couples over for a cookout. There must have been eight or ten people altogether. We barbequed and polished off a few cocktails, then after the sun went down we sat outside on the patio, talking. One couple, Devon and Gayle, decided to use our hot tub, so they went inside to get changed. Devon got changed first and came on out to the tub. Just as he got in, we heard Gayle cut loose with a god-awful scream. A couple of us jumped up and headed to the back door, but before we could get inside, out came Gayle, wearing nothing but her swimsuit bottoms. She was so hysterical she didn't even realize she wasn't what you would call decent. We grabbed a towel and wrapped it around her, and she stood there shaking and crying. It was a couple minutes before she could compose herself enough to talk. In the meantime, a couple guys went in the house to see if there was an intruder or something, but they didn't find anything out of order.

"After she calmed down," says Karla,

she told us she was in the bathroom getting changed to use the hot tub. She had bent over to pull up her swimsuit bottom, and when she straightened up again, this old man was standing over by the bathroom window, staring at her. That's when she took off running and screaming.

It was from this bathroom in Livonia, Michigan, that a female houseguest fled in terror, half dressed, upon seeing the ghost of the horrid old man.

After calming Gayle down, some of the guests began to playfully tease her about seeing "spooks," so Tom and Karla decided it was best to let Gayle off the hook and spill the beans about their ghost. They relayed the weird encounters they had been having over the past couple months, including the locked doors, the ghostly visits, and so on. That sort of changed the tone of the conversation from one of playful chiding to muted curiosity.

"Someone suggested we do a seance," says Karla,

but I nixed that idea right out of the gate. Then six or seven of them decided to do a ghosthunt and stuck their noses into every nook and cranny of our house—thank God it had just been cleaned. Nobody saw anything at all. All the while, Gayle was drinking one beer after another and just taking it all in. By the time the ghost hunt was finished, she was actually intrigued by it all and asked if she could come over and stay the night some time. We told her we'd be happy to have her, but we couldn't have any more half-naked hysterics or the neighbors would get the wrong idea about us.

Over the next couple of years, the haunting still manifested itself to Tom and Karla, but on a more sporadic basis. Every now and then they would catch a glimpse of a man scooting past a doorway or window. Sometimes they would experience cold spots for which they had no explanation. On a couple of occasions, they even found the refrigerator door open, usually in the morning right after they had gotten out of bed. Curiously, however, they were no longer locked out of the house. Then, about a year before the research into and writing of this chapter, things got active again. "My grandmother passed away about a year and a half ago," Karla says,

> and I kept one of the vases from the funeral service. We're Catholic, and this was a tall bronze vase with a crucifix attached to the front. I took it home after the funeral and put it on my bedroom dresser. When I got up the next morning, it was on the floor. It hadn't been knocked off or anything, because it was standing upright on the floor next to the dresser with the flowers and water still inside. It was just like someone had picked it up and set it there on purpose. Over the next few months it happened several more times. We never saw it happen—never even heard anything. After a while, we would just pick it up and put it back without giving it much thought. In fact, I really didn't think for a minute that it was the ghost of the old man doing it, I thought it was probably my grandmother.

Karla may have harbored that thought a bit prematurely. It seems one morning she got out of bed and the vase once again wasn't on the dresser. It was on the floor, only this time the flowers were strewn across the floor, and the vase lay all twisted and bent atop a soaked spot on the carpeting.

That vase was ruined. It looked like someone had

taken it and banged it with a hammer or twisted it in a vise. Like I said, it was made of bronze, and no way could anyone bang it up like that with their bare hands. What's really unsettling is that we didn't hear a thing all night.

Shortly after the twisted vase incident, Tom was in the basement drilling holes in some two-by-fours for a storage rack he was building. He says that all was well on that sunny afternoon until he got the strange sensation he wasn't alone down there. He says he looked up and over toward the corner of the basement and saw what looked like a man standing up against the foundation. Tom says it looked as though the man was emerging from the foundation itself, as he seemed to be "melting" in or out of it. He watched it for a minute or so, and then he said the figure seemed to pulsate back and forth, first coming out of the foundation a bit more, and then seeping back into it once again. After a short moment, it just faded away. After that, Tom says he rearranged his work area so he could finish the project without having to face that direction again.

There seems to be no logical explanation for the haunting of their home, and Tom and Karla aren't surprised at that. "How," asks Karla, "can you settle in with a logical explanation for something that doesn't make any sense?" Good question. Still, they've exhausted just about every explanation they can think of, logical or not. They've run the gamut of ghosthunting societies and psychics, entertained every interested relative or friend wishing to remark on the strange visitations, and consulted with clergy for some sort of spiritual understanding of it all. "Nothing really makes sense to us," says Tom.

The psychics talked about auras and emanations and life forms, but all they really seemed to be interested in was $50 a session. The ghosthunting society we called in turned out to be a few people with expensive film and electronic sensors of some type.

They talked about energy and magnetism and so forth, but it seemed like they already had their minds made up about us having a ghost before they even did anything. It's really hard to find people to take a serious look at this thing.

As this chapter was in its final editing phase, Karla phoned me. "Just thought you'd like to know," said she,

that the old man showed up in our kitchen last night. Tom was watching the Tigers play on TV and went to get a beer. He said the old guy was over by the back door, and when Tom looked straight at him, he disappeared.

According to Karla, Tom felt it reason enough for two beers. In fact, he now refers to the old man as the "two-beer" ghost, because once you encounter him, it takes more than one to calm yourself down again. Interesting. Maybe I should do away with the "Haunt Meter" and replace it with an "Imbibe Meter." A non-threatening ghost would rate a glass of wine; a spooky encounter, a stiff scotch on the rocks; and an all out fright-fest, a thorough, self-indulgent plastering.

Well, it's a thought.

11

The Ghost Who Growls

Location of Haunting: A single-family dwelling on Mackinac Island, a popular resort nudged between both of Michigan's peninsulas, surrounded by the waters of Lake Huron. The home in question belongs to year-round residents who prefer that their exact location not be given to the general public. The reason for this is quite simple. For much of the year the island is inundated with tourists, swelling its population to astronomical proportions. Having to deal with an extreme lack of privacy as folks invade nearly every nook and cranny of the island, the revelation of the correct location, and the subsequent flooding of nosy persons upon their abode, would not bode well for the family's well being.

Mackinac Island is easy to get to from anywhere in the state. From the Lower Peninsula, take I-75 north to Mackinac City, just below the bridge, and catch a ferry boat over to the island, where you will be held captive by its pristine beauty and scenic expanses until another ferry boat rescues you. From the U.P., take Highway 2 to St. Ignace and catch the ferry boat there.

Period of Haunting: As the family relates to me, this haunting has been going on for a couple of years and has only recently calmed down.

Date of Investigation: First contact with the haunting of "Fudge Island" was by telephone in the summer of 2001. Subsequent phone calls continued over the next several months.

Description of Location: Mackinac Island offers beautiful views of two of the Great Lakes—Huron and Michigan. It also offers the spectacular sight of the Mackinac Bridge, completed in 1957, finally hooking up the two peninsulas. The depth of beauty this island has to offer must be experienced to be believed. While there, check out the old British fort, with its whitewashed walls and original cannon. Then go buy some peanut butter fudge from a shop on Main Street. Take in a horse-and-carriage ride across the rolling hills and then go buy some almond mocha fudge. Stroll the largest covered porch you'll ever encounter—the porch of The Grand Hotel—and soak in the breathtaking beauty of the hotel's expansive gardens, and then go buy some chocolate walnut fudge. Rent a bicycle (automobiles are not permitted on the island) and take your time exploring the fascinating and historical spots dotted all over the island, and then go buy some vanilla pecan fudge. Get the picture?

The Haunt Meter: * * * *

Ernie and Lydia Gwynn (not their real names) have been full-time residents of Mackinac Island for a good many years. It takes a hardy soul and firm disposition to remain on the island during the cold season, as northern Michigan winters can be absolutely brutal on the island. As the lake is frozen over, there are no speedboats to cart denizens to the mainland at their every whim, so most folks just tough it out, although they maintain it's such a peaceful part of their lives, it's not difficult to do.

Virtually all the homes on Mackinac Island are historic, with the exception of those homes built since the beginning of the millionaire expansion in 1975. Ernie and Lydia occupy a narrow, two-story wood frame home with a terrific view (can there be any bad views there?). They love their old home and are quite mystified by the unseen presence who shows up every now and then to make their pulses skip along a little more rapidly than necessary.

"The first time we noticed anything," says Ernie,

> was about six or seven years back. We sometimes rent out a room or two to tourists who want to get away from all the noise and activity, and one morning one couple took me aside and asked why we didn't tell them the place had a ghost. I told them I wasn't aware of any such thing, and I meant it, but I don't think they believed me.

I asked Ernie, a man of strong muscles and stout character, what that couple complained about. "Well," he says,

> they claim they had turned in for the night and were just settling down in the bed when they heard a tapping noise on the wall behind the headboard. When I suggested it might have been some kind of animal in the wall, they said it couldn't have been, because they started tapping back to scare it off, and whenever they tapped, it would tap. If they tapped three times, so did it. It matched them tap for tap.

I asked Ernie if he offered to raise the rental fee for the added entertainment they had gotten, but he said the couple wasn't in a happy mood.

> I guess they thought it was fun at first, but when they started tapping in different sequences, and it did the same back, they started to get spooked. I wish they had come down and told us about it, I would like to have seen that for myself.

It wasn't long before Lydia and Ernie got a taste of the strangeness for themselves. One night, during the fall when things had quieted down considerably on the island, they were sitting in the living room when they heard something strange upstairs. "Ernie was watching television, and I was reading a paper," says Lydia.

> We both heard it at the same time, a sort of growling noise coming from somewhere upstairs. If you've ever

heard a raccoon when he's mad about something, it was sort of like that. We both went upstairs—Ernie first in case it was a raccoon—and the growling noise was louder. We couldn't for the life of us tell where it was coming from. It was like it was all around us everywhere we went. We did know it couldn't be a raccoon or any other animal, though, because it would first be in one room, and then the next. It would be behind you, and then all of a sudden it would be above you. It was pretty scary, but after a while it just went away.

The Gwynns were relieved when the growling dissipated, but after a few days it returned, this time more incessantly. "We were in the kitchen having our supper," says Ernie,

when we heard it again, this time sounding like it was coming from the living room. We sat real still for a while and listened. It growled for a bit, and then we heard a hissing noise. It sent chills up our spines. It was pretty cool outside, so the windows weren't open and so it couldn't have been coming from outdoors. In a minute or two it stopped, and we couldn't do anything but finish our meal.

Throughout that winter odd things began to accompany the growls and hisses. Doors would be found open that the Gwynns knew to be closed and locked earlier. The bathroom light would dim and then go very bright, and the smell of sewage would often fill one of the bedrooms, even though there was no trash anywhere in the house. "I thought at first an animal or mouse had died in the bedroom wall," says Lydia, "but the smell was only there for a few seconds at a time, and then all would be well again. Dead animals don't move, and they don't stink and then clear up that fast."

As if this weren't enough to give the good homeowners pause, they soon had to endure a more frightening experience. "This past winter [referring to the winter of 2000], we had gone to bed, and things hadn't happened for quite a long while," says Ernie.

> We started to hear that growling noise again, and we sort of froze. We laid there real still and listened, and it went away, but then we started hearing a raspy voice coming from the hallway outside the bedroom. It's the kind of voice you hear when someone has bad laryngitis and they're trying hard to talk in a loud whisper. At first we couldn't hear what it was trying to say, but then it got louder and louder. It kept saying something like, "You can't do that, you can't do that," over and over. Talk about scared! When it went away, it took all I could do to check out the house. I turned every light on and took my gun with me. Didn't find a thing, though.

I asked the Gwynns if they had any inkling of strange activity the first few years they resided in the home. They told me that everything had been normal and well for a long time, and that the weird happenings were relatively new. When I asked if it appeared that things were getting progressively worse, they indicated they thought it was for a while.

"It seems like just about the time things settle down, something else starts up," says Lydia.

> Ernie was off to a friend's house one day this past spring, and I was in the kitchen getting lunch ready. From behind me came this god-awful loud bang, and I turned around to see what it was, but there wasn't anything to see, everything looked normal to me. Just then, the cupboard door next to the stove, the lower one not the upper one, started swinging open and slamming shut really fast. "Bang, bang, bang," it went, just like somebody or something was really mad about something. I was just paralyzed with fear and took off out of there. Then it just stopped. Not long after that Ernie came home for lunch and I told him what had happened. I know he would have never believed me if we hadn't already had those weird noises going on, but he could tell I was serious. He looked at the cupboard door, and there wasn't any reason it should have been doing that.

I wondered aloud how anyone could stand living in a home that seemed to be suddenly invaded by what appeared to be an angry spirit or two. They assured me it wasn't easy and that there were moments when they felt they had to get away, but it was their home. They had never had trouble before and they thought maybe it would go away just as fast as it had shown up. No such luck.

"We had friends over for cards and beer one night," says Lydia,

> and everyone was drinking and having a good time. All of a sudden my girlfriend shouts out, "What the heck was that?" I looked over just in time to see what looked like the shadow of someone moving up the stairs. Before I could say anything, we all started hearing what sounded like a distant howling from up there. It just kept going on and on without a break for air for two or three minutes. Then we heard something pounding around in the bedroom, and the two guys headed up there to check it out. When they came down they said they couldn't hear or see anything, but they were glad they were together up there.

Fed up with their growling, raspy-voiced ghoul, Ernie and Lydia took their friends' advice and called in a minister from a church on the mainland. "We didn't want anyone on the island knowing about this, so we got hold of a minister not far from Mackinac City," says Ernie.

> When we told him what was happening, he offered to come over right away. He was really helpful, but we asked him not to tell anyone about this, so I can't tell you his name. Anyway, he went through the house, and said a prayer in every single room. Then he started reading from the Bible and demanded that whatever unclean spirit was there had to go. You know, I'm not one to really believe in all this stuff, but since he's left we haven't had a single incident, not one.

The Gwynns are grateful it's over now and sincerely

hope the haunting of their home won't pick up again some day. Like Ernie says,

It takes a certain type of person to live on the island year-round, and we don't mind it a bit. But we don't think we have the kind of personality it takes to put up with whatever was in our house.

The statue of a Union soldier guards the graves at Manchester Cemetery.

12

This Cemetery Talks

Location of Haunting: A cemetery on the outskirts of the small town of Manchester, Michigan, about twenty minutes west of Ann Arbor.

Period of Haunting: The information in this story has only recently come to my attention, but the persons involved, who wish to remain anonymous, insist they have encountered paranormal activity for a few years now. They vigorously maintain that they scarcely make a visit without something strange taking place in their midst.

Date of Investigation: This tale was told to me in the early winter of 2001–2002. As of this writing, I have found a bit of time to try a few tape recordings of my own amongst the tombstones and crypts.

Description of Location: Manchester is a beautiful and remarkably well-maintained small town about twenty minutes east of Jackson, and also about twenty minutes west of Ann Arbor. Many splendid Victorian-style homes pepper some of the streets, and there's a restful little park situated just off the town square. From either east or west, you can travel the I-94 corridor to the M-52 exit, then guide your hood ornament south. Within a few minutes you will enter the town of Manchester. At the four-way stop, turn right and pass through town, being certain to watch your speed, as the local constabulary dogmatically enforces the 25-MPH speed limit. As you begin to leave town, look to your right and you'll behold a gorgeous (yes, cemeteries can certainly be gorgeous) cemetery. There is a large statue of a Union soldier, lighted at night, to commemorate those brave young boys who gave their lives in the Civil War.

While in Manchester, check out the antique shops and perhaps drop by the local Dairy Queen, season permitting, for a frozen treat. If your stomach requires more substantial sustenance, next to the Dairy Queen is a quaint restaurant with a terrific menu. It's the sort of building one would suspect to be haunted, but, thus far, no ghostly phenomena have been reported. Manchester is home to what they term, "The Famous Chicken Barbeque," an event taking place over a couple of days in July, enveloping the entire area with the aromatic wafting of char-broiled fowl. In the summer of 2002, they kicked off their inaugural art fair, an event certain to shed new light on an old town. Should you decide fall is the time to check out the ghostly graveyard, be sure to take a tour down Austin Road (the same road that fronts the cemetery), heading west toward Napoleon. The fields, forests, and farmhouses offer truly magnificent explosions of color.

The Haunt Meter: * * *

I have no idea why cemeteries so captivate those folks who ascribe to the presence of the paranormal in everyday life. I cannot tell you how many times someone has come up to me and inquired whether or not I have "checked out" a particular cemetery. Invariably, these persons spin their yarns about local last resting spots harboring the wispy remains of those long removed from this work-a-day world. To hear people tell it, just about every cemetery in Michigan—and I suppose elsewhere, as well—is home to the eerie noises and shadowy mists that they believe constitute proof of the presence of a ghost or two.

My first response to these folks is a pragmatic one— why on earth would any self-respecting spirit choose to hang out around a bunch of cold tombstones after they're gone? I can easily understand the theory that ghosts appear to haunt the places or people that were near and dear to their hearts, but a graveyard? It would seem that a ghost with emotional connections to anything at all would rather be someplace else. Houses often seem to be the focal (and sometimes vocal) point of ghostly activity, and for good reason. Most people are quite attached to where they once lived and created pleasant memories. The major events of their lives have often been celebrated in their homes with friends and family. So it's no surprise the dead roam those corridors composed of brick and mortar, lumber and lath. But a cemetery? It just doesn't make sense to me. But when dealing with ghosts, what does?

Still, there are those who insist that cemeteries are great places to encounter active spirits. They maintain myriad reasons why the unsettled dead inexplicably flit about the headstones—maybe they are still strongly drawn to their physical bodies; perhaps the trauma emanating from grief holds emotional sway over them (after all, this is often the last place folks cry in concert over you); or possibly they experience the kinship of other spirits in such a setting (not the sort of place I intend to commune with my buddies upon my demise, but then again, I'm not dead yet). At any rate, many a gallant ghosthunter has laid claim to paranormal experiences while tiptoeing through the tulips, as well as the the marble and limestone.

Becky and Galen are such folk. When they first approached me at a book signing in Jackson, Michigan, I admit I was a bit more than skeptical of their tale. After all, I knew the cemetery well and I had never heard any such tale before. Yet they appeared to be respectable people, clean cut and thirty-ish, articulate and sincere. I lent them my ear as I continued to inscribe books to this person or to that person.

Becky and Galen live, if my memory is correct,

somewhere in the vicinity of the Norvell/Wolf Lake area (informed later that this tale was to end up in my next book, they were understandably vague about their exact whereabouts). Sharing an interest in paranormal phenomena, and an unquenchable desire to experience firsthand the presence of spirits, they set out to explore ways to encounter the dead. For them, Ouija board sessions simply ended in a disjointed barrage of mixed messages, and meditation sort of, well, put them to sleep. Since these and other forms of amateur spectral detection left them without a good case of the shivers, they were about to give up on ever connecting with the spirits of the physically dead, when they by chance heard a radio station interview with a small band of ghosthunters who spoke of their successes while traipsing around graveyards in the dead of night.

"The whole interview was fascinating," says Becky.

> We were coming back from a trip to Pennsylvania, and it was well after midnight. The more we listened, the creepier it got. They talked about how they would go into cemeteries with tape recorders and try to record the voices of the dead.

This was something Becky and Galen had never thought of trying, and the idea seemed to strike a bright chord for them.

> They said they would go to the cemetery at night because that's when it's the quietest, and they'd find a spot they felt comfortable with, and they would turn on their recorders and just let them run. Sometimes they'd get voices on the tape—and they played some of their tapes on the radio. You could hear people whispering and talking. It never lasted long, and most of the time you didn't know for sure what they were saying, but they were voices, all right. Sometimes, the live people would ask questions and they'd get answers from the ghosts, and one time a couple of the women there were joking about something, and they recorded a laugh that wasn't from one of their group.

While cemeteries are not the most cheerful of places for most people to visit when they have a free evening, it's at least nice to know the dead have a sense of humor, or at least the civility to chuckle politely at one's jokes. But, I digress. Let's let Galen have a turn.

"The instant we heard that radio interview," says Galen,

> we both just felt this was the technique for us. We sort of figured that if the ghosts want to speak, maybe they'd be willing to let themselves be recorded. And maybe they do speak, but so many of us just can't hear them, like we're not on the same wavelength or something. For all we knew, they had been trying to communicate with us for a long time, but we couldn't hear them. Anyway, we decided to use this tape recorder technique.

Galen and Becky say it's really pretty simple to get started, that you don't need a great deal of expensive equipment. They strode into their local Radio Shack store and picked up a cassette recorder. As they explained it to me, it's best to use a recorder with an external microphone, as the internal microphone system will pick up the sounds of the cassette wheels turning, or produce a "hissing" noise that interferes with spectral conversation (I'm not sure Radio Shack makes a recorder specifically for cemetery prowling, but you can ask). While they cautioned me not to buy a cheap outfit, they maintained they only invested about $75 in their ghost-gear: $40 for the recorder, $20 for the microphone, and the balance on fresh tapes. "Don't use used tapes," says Galen, "because if you record over something, you might just be picking up some of what was already on the tape."

The gist of the operation goes like this: take your gear to your local cemetery, preferably at night when all is quiet, set up your equipment and just keep quiet while it runs. Then, sit in a quiet place and listen to the tapes. The tip I received here is to listen through

Entry into the haunted cemetery in Manchester, Michigan.

headphones, and turn the sound up as loud as you can stand it. What you'll hear will be what is supposedly known as "white noise," the sound all tapes produce to some degree when they are left to run with nothing to record. Listen closely, because usually what you'll get within the white noise is whispering, although sometimes folks experience voices with much more clarity. (Author's note: it's always best to alert the local police to your midnight foray. They regularly check out cemeteries after dark as they are favorite spots for romantic trysts, which may be the main cause of spectral tongue-wagging. While the police may think you're a bit off your nut, they'll normally give the nod to your less than ordinary request to remain there.)

Such is the procedure used by Becky and Galen. "We were really excited," she says,

> the first time we went to the cemetery. We picked the Manchester Cemetery because it wasn't too far away, and because it's such a beautiful place. We got there

about 11 P.M. and found a nice spot just over the hill, away from Austin Road so we wouldn't pick up too much traffic noise. Then we just set the recorder on a tombstone and let it run. We figured it would take forty-five minutes to finish, so we tiptoed away and sat in the car. Then we took the tape home and listened to it under the headphones.

Actually, it was Galen who was first to don the headphones, shortly after returning home. "I could hear the noise from us turning the tape recorder on, and I could hear us whispering and then walking away," says Galen.

Then there was just a bunch of continuous white noise. Sometimes you could make out the sound of a car passing by in the distance, but mostly it was just that white noise. Then, about twenty-five minutes into the tape, I heard someone say, "He's over there," and I just about freaked. I mean, it was clear as a bell, just like he was talking to somebody else. I tore off those headphones and just about screamed for Becky to come and hear it. She put the phones on and heard it too—at first I couldn't tell if she was scared or excited. She just started yelling, "Oh, my God, oh, my God," over and over.

After wresting the headphones away from his wife, Galen says he barely breathed while listening to the rest of the tape, hopeful of another ghostly outburst. He didn't have to wait very long. "I was just under the phones another three or four minutes when I heard another voice," says Galen. "It sounded like it said, 'I'm lonely,' but when Becky listened to it, she said she thought it said, 'It's cold here.' We couldn't tell if it was the same voice both times."

Galen and Becky told me they've returned to the Manchester Cemetery on several occasions and have had luck in recording spectral soundings about half the time. "We've taped a woman crying," says Becky,

and what sounds like a couple of different men, too. I

can't tell if they're trying to talk to us through the tape or if we're just picking up bits of conversation not intended for us. Anyway, none of the voices seem to be directed at us. Sometimes we can make out what they're saying, but other times it's like listening to someone far off, close enough to hear a voice but too far away to understand what they're saying all the time. And at least once, while we were recording, we both saw what appeared to be a light, bluish, sort of smoky image float by one of the tombstones. It only lasted a quick second or two, but we both know we saw it. It really makes you feel weird, like you're not alone whenever you're there. I don't think I'll ever feel the same as I used to in any cemetery.

I've driven past the Manchester Cemetery many times in the past thirty-five years, and, although I have never driven into it, I have often thought to myself how pristine and peaceful it is. I particularly enjoy the Union soldier, resplendent in his blue uniform, gallantly standing guard over the tombstones, gazing stoically out toward Austin Road. Never had I given a thought to the possibility that it could be inundated with ghosts. In fact, to me, its well-tailored beauty would seem to inherently defy the presence of spectral activity. After all, aren't ghosts supposed to inhabit only the dregs of society's cemeteries?

I set out one fine winter's day in early 2002 to check out the ghostly whisperings for myself. Normally, I would reserve this sort of activity for the spring of the year, but with record high temperatures spreading across the Great Lakes State, I steered my Mazda down Austin Road and up into the cemetery, cresting the small rise in the terrain. Although it was daylight, I reasoned that if any spirits had anything to say, there would be no real reason for them to feel the need for twilight to encroach upon the landscape before speaking up. Thus, I spent the early afternoon hours sitting in my car, basking in the warm sunlight washing through the windshield, tape recorder silently running atop a marble grave marker. The window was cracked open a bit, so I could keep track of outside noises such as passing cars, noting the times of such intrusions on a notepad, so that when I played back the tape I'd know which sounds could easily be accounted for. I must admit I felt a bit silly at first, and sincerely hoped no one would drive through on their way to visit a dear departed one and behold what would certainly appear to be some sort of nutcase parked among the tombstones, silently and privately engaged in who-knows-what.

After having filled both sides of my tape with who-knew-what, I plugged my headphones into the recorder, turned up the volume as loud as my middle-aged ears could stand it and began to listen for anything out of the ordinary. After ninety minutes of dedicated listening (possibly interspersed with a bit of catnapping), I discovered the only thing out of the ordinary was me, parked in a cemetery, listening to absolutely nothing through a set of headphones.

Just because I had no luck in the Manchester Cemetery doesn't mean others have not been successful. In fact, I have heard one of the tapes Becky and Galen made and, if I choose to take them at their word, it certainly appears someone is trying to make their presence known amid the statues and markers and crypts. They claim a couple friends of theirs have tried the same experiment with results equal to theirs.

Did I visit the cemetery at the wrong time of day? Should I have purchased Sony tapes in lieu of TDK? Or am I just one of those guys who unconsciously blocks this sort of thing out of my personal realm of possibilities for whatever reason? Who knows? Just because I didn't have any luck the first time out doesn't mean I won't have luck on a repeat visit.

In conclusion, I leave this one up to you, gentle readers, to decide. Perhaps you should take it upon yourselves to visit this lovely little final resting place and check it out yourself for paranormal rumblings. Take along your recorders and maybe a video camera as well. Quite often, according to some folks, where there are voices, there are images, both of which are not readily apparent to human eyes and ears, but able to etch themselves upon the tapes of our newfangled electrical recording devices. And if you get anything positive, I'd like to hear about it. For that matter, if you have any cemetery images or noises from any cemetery at all, I'm open-minded enough to examine them for myself.

13

Stay Out of Those Woods

Location of Haunting: A Christmas tree farm, covering many acres, somewhere in Michigan's Lower Peninsula. I am not at liberty to provide the address.

Period of Haunting: The haunting in question may have actually existed for decades. Judging from the strangeness of the tale and the very nature of the beast, there is actually no way of knowing just when the strange activities began; they most certainly continue, in a more contained form, to this day.

Date of Investigation: April, 2002.

Description of Location: This haunting is not so much associated with a person or a specific place as it is an area. As Christmas trees are the source of income for the persons involved, it would be quite improper for me to disclose the location of this haunting. My enthrallment with ghosts is no reason to cause harm to another's livelihood. Respectful readers of this genre are expected to agree with me here. The owners of the property and business in question don't need droves of ghost afficionados staking out the area making their lives any more miserable.

The Haunt Meter: * * * *

This may be one of the strangest tales I've encountered in all my "ghosthunting" days. In fact, the entity in-

volved here may not fit the generalized description of a
ghost at all. It is obviously not human, is quite territo-
rial, and wreaks havoc upon anyone who dares to
infringe on its "territory." Intrigued? Then pry open your
mind, and let's take a walk in the woods.

I received an e-mail, as well as a subsequent telephone call, from a very highly respected professional
person residing in one of Detroit's more upscale sub-
urbs. While I cannot divulge this individual's name or
occupation, I assure you I am impressed enough by her
position and esteem within the community to immediately take what I became privy to as truth. In fact,
should this individual's identity become public knowledge, one fine career could go down the proverbial sewer
pipe. Having this much to lose is a good indication as to
the viability of the story given me. We shall refer to this
individual as "Emily."

Emily has enjoyed a friendship spanning thirty years
with Susan and Doug Myers (names altered to protect
their interests). The three of them attended school
together and kept in close contact with one another
during their college days. As had been expected all
those years ago, Susan and Doug married. Tiring of the
hectic lifestyle often associated with suburbia, they
purchased a Christmas tree farm far from the madden-
ing crowd. They had two young sons, and the idea of a
country life meshed well with the values they wished to
impart to their youngsters.

Susan and Doug had barely moved into their new
homestead when they began to notice how often they
and their sons were becoming ill. It began with what
they thought to be the usual cold and flu bugs. After
several months of visits to the local clinic and emer-
gency rooms, they grew more than just a little puzzled
by their frequent maladies.

Physical illnesses were not the only plague they
began to encounter. Susan and Doug, normally in-

tensely devoted to one another, began to spat a bit now and then, something quite foreign to their relationship. Each was becoming a bit moody, and this moodiness appeared to be growing somewhat with the passing of time. "They had moved quite a distance away," says Emily, "so most of my visiting was done by means of e-mail and telephone. Over time, I could sense the tension, and I was already aware of the nagging illnesses."

Emily decided a trip to see her lifelong friends was in order, and she set aside some time from her demands and responsibilities to spend a few days with them. "It had been a long drive," says Emily,

> and I arrived late. It's truly a beautiful area way up there, and I was looking forward to a nice visit and some quiet time to relax. But as soon as I got out of the car I could sense something wasn't right. Although I live in the city, I've also spent a good deal of time in the country with relatives, so I'm not one to be put off by remoteness. Still, it just seemed to me that I was being watched by something. Susan and Doug had waited up for me and the porch light was on. All the way to the door I could feel this malevolent thing staring at me, to the point where I couldn't wait to get into the house.

Aside from the rather inhospitable welcoming she received out in the driveway, Emily's visit began quite well. They stayed up into the early hours of the morning, sipping tea and chattering away, overcoming the vacuum created in their lives by past separation. The next day, after a late and lingering breakfast, she was given the grand tour of her friends' estate. "It's truly an expansive holding," says Emily.

> There are acres and acres of trees to tend. Behind the tree farm is a small rise leading up to an expanse of woods, mostly hardwoods. Doug and Sue own a great portion of that woods as well. For most of the tour we used their SUV, stopping along the way every now and then to get out and walk around a bit. I have to admit

that the scent of the evergreens and sounds of all the nature were pleasant enough, but I still had a strong sense of foreboding, as though I needed to keep looking over my shoulder.

Later that evening, Emily was disconcerted to realize there was a strain in the relationship between Doug and Sue. Where she had once viewed them as the ideal couple, very much in love with one another, they would now snap at each other over the slightest irritations. After several glasses of wine, it came out that Doug had not been feeling well as of late and had begun a series of medical tests at the behest of his physician. As if that weren't enough, Emily discovered that one of their sons, David, was having what appeared to be chronic bouts of asthmatic-like breathing, brought on, so they believed, by allergies, something he had never experienced before moving out of the city.

Long after midnight, the conversation having drained away with the wine, everyone went off to bed. "My room," says Emily,

was the guestroom upstairs. It was in the back south-west corner of the house, with windows overlooking the tree farm and the tree-lined rise beyond. All the while I prepared for bed, I had the strong sense once again of being watched. I recall I lay in bed for several minutes, trying to wash through the feelings of the evening, and I got the strong urge to look outside, as though something was pulling me toward the window. I pulled back the curtain and looked outside. The moon was quite full and the sky was clear, so I had a splendid view out over the tree farm. As I scanned the ridge beyond, I became almost violently afraid, as though something out there was stalking not only me, but everyone on the property. The sense I got was that it was not human, but some sort of twisted animal form, something one would not normally associate with our world at all. I sensed it had intelligence of some degree, but that it was evil.

The next day together was rather uneventful and

somewhat more pleasurable for everyone. They dined in town together, lingering until close over cocktails. "Doug and Sue seemed as though they were back to normal," says Emily.

> Then, as we drove back home, it seemed the closer we got, the more edgy everyone seemed to become. Doug drove the sitter home, and Sue and I made small talk for a while. Then I asked her if she was comfortable in her new life outside the city. I remember her saying to me, "I thought I would be," and then changing the subject.

Upon retiring for the evening, Emily once again felt the overwhelming urge to look out the window, but fought it off, telling herself she was letting her imagination get the best of her. The next morning, however, as she packed her things for the return trip to the city, the foreboding returned. "I was back upstairs gathering my things," says Emily,

> and it were as though a rush of fear blew into the room. I was instantly terrified, but I still didn't know exactly why. I just knew that kind of fear was being generated from something, and I felt I had to know more.

After helping to pack her car, Doug left for a meeting with his accountant, leaving the two women to say their goodbyes alone. "I could sense Sue was not herself and really didn't want me to go," says Emily,

> and I really did want an excuse to go back out into the tree farm, so I suggested a walk before leaving. It was a gorgeous morning. All the birds were singing and the sun was nicely warm. We walked through the rows of trees, chatting away about this and that. I noticed that the further into the trees we walked, the quieter things had become. Eventually, we reached the edge of the farm, about one hundred yards from the wooded ridge, and the beautiful day now seemed somewhat remote. I recall I could hear Sue's voice, but that was all. The birds weren't singing any more and everything seemed

Author, Gerald Hunter, on the ridge of a tree farm where a "beast" has been seen roaming about.

strangely still. As Sue spoke we both faced the ridge. That's when I finally saw what had been terrifying me since the moment I had arrived. Just outside the edge of the tree line, at the very crest of the ridge, was this animal figure. I say animal figure because it really wasn't an animal, but it really wasn't human either. It was sort of like a centaur, but stood on two legs with hooves. It was angularly muscular and quite fluid in movement. It was covered in fur and even though it was still pretty far away, I felt it was evil incarnate. It watched us as we stood there, yet after a moment or two I realized Sue wasn't seeing it at all.

It ought to be noted that Emily has been prone all her life to psychic phenomena. She has encountered the spirits of the dead, both relatives and strangers, on many occasions and has long ago accepted the fact that we are not alone in this earthly world of ours. "I knew Sue wasn't seeing this thing," says Emily,

because she wasn't open to such encounters. Eventually, I could no longer hear her voice, but I could receive what seemed like thought patterns coming from this animal. The sense I got was that it was enraged there were people encroaching upon its domain. Sue and Doug had recently enlarged their holdings, bringing the farm quite near the ridge where the beast was now standing. The feeling I had was that whatever this thing was, it had a certain range it covered and protected as its own. Because Sue and Doug were threatening its perceived territory, it was retaliating by making their lives miserable, even to the point of inflicting serious illness upon them. I watched it for a couple of minutes, and then it turned and stealthily slid back into the woods and out of sight.

Emily was now very much frightened for her friends. After returning home, she spent several days giving thought as to how to share her encounter with them. However, Doug's health soon took a turn for the worse, and Emily thought it best not to add any further strain to their already tenuous condition.

Emily was now frantic for the safety of her friends. Certain she had to do something, she decided to take matters into her own hands.

"I decided to stop by," says Emily,

> but it was when I knew Sue wasn't home. I entered the edge of the woods by the entry road in the back of their property and once again strongly sensed the evil creature that lived there. I meditated for spiritual strength, and as I did I could feel this thing getting more and more enraged with me. I did my best to surround the tree farm with positive energy, and after about an hour or so, I sensed the rage of the beast diminishing. Soon, I was confident it was contained and that it would no longer be a bother to Sue and Doug. I believe it's confined to the woods and can't venture any further. At least I hope so.

This author realizes this is not your average ghost story, but then, what is? It does, however, have a happy ending. Doug recovered from his illness, inexplicably showing no further signs of what was ailing him. Young David seems to have adjusted to the area much better, and his breathing is easily under control with inhalers. But I imagine there is one ticked-off beast prowling around out there amongst the oaks.

14

Mirror, Mirror, on the Wall

Location of Haunting: A rambling, two-story wood frame home, decades old in its appearance, located on Grove Street, just off the main artery passing through the city of Midland. As is quite usual with the loss of privacy in today's world, the family wishes no exact address be disclosed. A little good ghosthunting of your own may suffice to discover the house's whereabouts, and if you are successful, at least refrain from treading upon their porch steps. A good ghosthunter is a polite ghosthunter.

To arrive in the vicinity of the haunted dwelling, take I-75 north from Flint until you reach US-10, then head west. In a few minutes you'll pass Auburn (check out the McDonald's at this exit, as the owner always has a classic hot rod or two inside the restaurant). The next city is Midland. Continue toward the downtown area until you reach Haley Street and turn right. Take an immediate turn to the left at Grove. You will then be driving down the street on which the haunted house sits.

Period of Haunting: Although the intensity of the haunting covered the years 2000 through early 2002, strange incidents had been noticed by family members for many years prior.

Date of Investigation: The initial contact for this story was received just after the release of my first book.

E-mails and phone calls were initiated in mid-2001, and my first visit to the home took place in the early spring of 2002.

Description of Location: Midland, Michigan, is, for the most part, an upscale community near the western edge of the Thumb. It is peacefully tucked away somewhat between Mt. Pleasant on the west and Saginaw on the east, southeast. It is often referred to as one of the tri-cities, the other two being Saginaw and Bay City, and is considered by many to be the most desirable of the threesome in which to live. Midland is home to the Dow Chemical Company, which is a major employer in the area. Its downtown is quite well-kept, dotted with interesting stores and restaurants. There are a great many public parks in Midland, offering serene settings in which to relax and compose oneself after a hard day. If you're looking for an interesting landmark, try the "Tridge," so dubbed because, even though it is one bridge, it has the appearance of being three bridges, each section crossing a different part of the breaks of the Tittabawassee River. Just follow the "Tridge" signs along the route through town. Also of interest in Midland are the Herbert H. Dow Historical Museum and the Automobile Hall of Fame. Midland is located about two hours north of Detroit, off the I-75 corridor. As a side note, there is a theater multiplex, rather new, near the Midland Mall. It is reputed by many residents to harbor a few ghosts of its own, as they claim it was built on haunted land. I've yet to check it out, so I guess it's fair game to any of you dear readers.

The Haunt Meter: * * * *

I must admit that I am both drawn to, and repulsed by, the horrifying nature of this haunting. I am drawn to it the same way I am drawn to any ghostly phenomena—with a strong sense of wonderment and fascination. I am repulsed by this haunting because it hits far too closely to a terrifying incident of my childhood.

When I was about seven tender years of age, way back in the very late 1950s, I was invited to spend the night at my paternal grandparents home in Garden City. It was a small, tidy home staked out on the corner of Merriman and Barton Streets, just south of Ford Road. I loved my grandparents dearly. Grandma Hunter was a nurse and patched me up on more than one occasion after a rowdy session of outdoor roughhousing. My grandfather was a jack-of-all-trades, the sort of man who could do just about anything, and usually do it pretty well. Truth be told, one of the reasons they were my favorites was that they always kept ladyfinger buttercreme cookies in the cookie jar, and their refrigerator always boasted neat rows of 7-UP and Vernor's Ginger Ale. But, as usual, I digress.

On the night in question, I had eaten my evening treat of cookies and soda pop. Darkness had blanketed the neighborhood, and I had donned my favorite Davy Crockett pajamas in an effort to stave off homesickness. As I was wont to do, I asked dear Grandma if I could stay up and watch a little television. As it was already fast approaching 10 P.M., I knew I was pushing my luck, but I also knew that grandparents possess a softer heart than mere parents do. Lo and behold, I was granted one additional hour.

As I flipped the channel selector first one way and then the other (this was way before remote controls made us all lazy), I finally chose a program I had always wanted to see, but which had heretofore been forbidden me by my parents. With Grandma and Grandpa off in the kitchen enjoying their evening coffee (this was also way before folks made the connection between caffeine and sleeplessness), I spread myself out on the living room floor for my first experience with *Boris Karloff Presents*, a program of macabre tales from the master of the sinister himself.

At first, the show was simply one big letdown. All I saw was a beautiful blonde's reflection in a mirror as she applied her makeup and brushed her hair. All the while she primped and pampered herself, someone was pounding on her front door, demanding entry under the guise they were concerned about her, as she hadn't been seen outside the house in weeks. Boring stuff to a seven-year-old.

As the program neared its denouement, I had pretty much grown tired of seeing this blonde beauty's mirror image. Then, just about the time I decided Boris Karloff held nothing for me, the camera suddenly moved off the woman's image in the mirror and onto her actual face, which was craggy and old and hideous. Caught off guard, I was literally jolted up off the floor in terror. While my heart pounded and adrenalin begged me to do something, anything, Karloff's face suddenly flashed onto the screen and his famous lisp spewed forth something like, "Many people trust mirrors to show them what they really look like, but the truth is, mirrors lie!" Well, that was it. I haven't been comfortable looking into a mirror ever since. To this day, I expect to innocently gaze into one only to discover some tortured ghoulish facade gazing back at me.

And that is why this haunting haunts me.

Ginger and Mark moved into the house on Grove Street several years ago. Mark works at one of the major factories dotting the Saginaw landscape, and Ginger is a homemaker. Between them, they have three children from two marriages. Both are amiable people, natives to the general area. Except for their haunting, they are not unlike most other people in their part of Michigan—they love the outdoors and frequent the woods and streams whenever possible.

The rather unnatural encounters began for them several years ago, shortly after moving into their home. Little oddities were taking place, such as kitchen knick-knacks being rearranged during the night, hallway lights turning themselves on when there was no one around, and bathroom faucets spewing forth water when no human hands had turned on the taps. These things alone would give one pause, if not question whether their personal sanity was slipping a gear or two. "It started out kind of slow," says Ginger, "and then, after we'd been here a while, things started to pick up."

It's often easy for people to pass off such unaccounted for events as oversights on their part, but it's also easy for some folks to chalk up any old kind of oddity to ghostly presences. Some folks don't want their home to be haunted; others will claim it's inhabited with spooks even when it clearly is not. Ginger and Mark would prefer they had no ghosts and lived for quite some time in deep denial of their ethereal guests until Ginger came literally face-to-face with one. "The first time I knew for certain that we had a ghost in the house was about two years ago," she says.

> It was a Monday afternoon, and I was just going around doing my housecleaning. I had just finished doing up some dishes and started a load of wash. Just as I did, I remembered there were some dirty towels upstairs I had forgotten about. I went upstairs and into the bathroom. I picked up the towels, and as I passed the sink I stopped to grab the washcloth that was there. I happened to glance into the bathroom mirror, and there was this face staring back at me from what seemed to be inside the mirror. It was a woman's face, and it was right next to the image of my own face. In fact, my face partially melted into the side of her face. She was staring right at me. It scared me so bad that I took off running all the way downstairs. I sat on the couch just really breathing hard, trying to get my wits about me. I was so scared it was like I didn't even want to move. Finally, I pulled myself together and got up the courage to leave the living room. I put the dirty towels in the washing machine and sort of tiptoed back

The bathroom mirror in Midland, Michigan,
where nasty faces peer back at folks.

to the bottom of the stairway. I just stood there, listening real close, but I couldn't hear anything but the washing machine. Then I went back into the living room and laid down on the couch for a while. I still had a lot of housework to do, but I was really shook. It wasn't until Mark came home from work around four o'clock that I started to feel better.

Ginger had no reservations about telling her husband of her encounter in the bathroom. "She was really shook," says Mark.

I knew she wasn't making anything up or that she just thought she saw something. She was too afraid at first to even go back upstairs. Finally, after about two hours, she agreed to go up there with me. I mean, she had to go up there again sometime, so it was best to go with me. But when we went back upstairs, of course there wasn't anything up there and the bathroom was fine.

It took a while for Ginger to go back into that particular bathroom with any degree of comfortableness. On each trip, she'd fully expect to see that face staring back at her from the mirror, but all seemed to be well again. "Every time I'd go in there," she says,

I'd do everything I could to avoid looking in that mirror, but at the same time it was like I had to look, so I'd take a real quick glance. It's like you don't want to see anything, but you have to make sure you won't see anything. It's hard to explain.

After the passage of several weeks, Ginger's experience with the bathroom mirror slowly seeped its way down into her unconscious mind and she managed to resume her daily routine without fear of unearthly interruptions. Such as is often the case with ghosts, just when you think it's safe to go back into the bathroom, they pop out at you once again. "I had all but forgotten what had happened to me," says Ginger,

and Mark and I were getting ready to go out for the evening—you know, the dinner-and-a-movie routine. I was in the bathroom fixing my hair. I have some pretty expensive perfume I use for special occasions, and I sprayed some of it on. I opened the vanity drawer and put it back, and when I looked up again, there was that same face again. I started screaming and screaming and I ran down the stairs. Mark didn't know what was up and thought maybe I'd hurt myself or something, but when I told him what happened, he ran up there, but he didn't see anything. I couldn't get out of the house fast enough, but even then I really didn't have much of a good time—all I could think about was having to go back home and maybe seeing that awful face again.

That "awful face," as Ginger describes it, seems to belong to a woman of about sixty. According to Ginger, she has deep-set dark eyes and wrinkles crease her entire face. Her hair is askew and is mostly light gray. Her eyebrows are heavy and her mouth is always partially open. Ginger says it feels like she's trying to burn a hole through you the way she stares at you.

It's hard to enjoy your home when you're terrified to be alone there. At the same time, it's your home, and you're reluctant to just pack up and leave for sunnier slopes. Not unlike many others who have had altercations with ghosts, Ginger started to convince herself that it wasn't the house that was being visited by nasty apparitional faces, but that maybe it was she who really had the problem. She entertained the thought that she might be cracking up and played with the idea of seeing a doctor or psychologist for an assessment of her emotional health. It was right about then that confirmation of the haunting came crashing in on them.

"Ginger went to visit her sister over near Sanford," says Mark,

and I stayed at home because I had to work. I got home around five, and then went out to dinner by myself. I came back home before eight and started puttering around the house and yard. After dark, I watched television until about eleven. I was going to catch the news, but first I wanted a Pepsi, so I went into the kitchen and got one from the fridge. When I came back into the living room, there's this small mirror we have next to the front door. It has three or four small hooks on the bottom of it to hang hats or coats from, but it's really more just decoration than anything else. Anyway, just as I started to go by it, something kind of caught my eye. I looked at the mirror, and there was this other guy's reflection in there with mine. You know, usually whenever someone's really scared you hear about how they just take off running. Man, I couldn't move. I was just froze, I was so scared. I was looking straight at this guy. He was an older guy, and his cheeks were sort of sunk in and he had gray stubble all over his face. I sort of like blinked, and he was just gone. I know it was stupid, but I went and got my shotgun and sat in the living room for a long time before finally going up to bed.

When Ginger returned home a couple days later from her sister's house, she was practically elated that her husband had seen a ghost, too, even if it was a different ghost from hers. "I knew it wasn't just me," says she, "but the real question then was just who were these people?"

One thing I've discovered since writing books on paranormal activity is just how many organizations dealing with ghosts and hauntings—professional and otherwise—exist in our society. They seem to be almost as prevalent as the ghosts they're tracking down. Therefore, it came as no surprise to me when Ginger informed me that she and her husband brought in a team of amateur ghosthunters to check out their abode. "They were really pretty nice people," says Ginger,

> but the impression I got was that they had already made up their minds about us having a ghost before they even arrived. I mean, after listening to our stories, they started telling us what they thought was going on even before they did any looking around. They told us

The entryway of Ginger and Mark's home. Mirrors that once hung on both sides of the door were taken down due to ghosts.

there were probably a lot of spirits in the house and that I was probably a magnet for them. What they had to say was pretty interesting, but I don't consider myself a magnet, and if there are truly ghosts in my house, then how come they only show up in the mirrors?

One of the nice things this amateur crew offered their terrified hosts was the name of a local woman who was purported to be psychic. Ginger and Mark held on to the card with her name on it for several weeks before phoning her. "We weren't going to call her at all," says Mark, but then the activity stepped up enough to where we'd finally had enough. My mother was over one night, and she went upstairs to use the bathroom because I was in the one downstairs. She says that when she went in, the door just seemed to slam shut when she barely touched it. When she got ready to leave the bathroom, she said the door wouldn't open. It's the kind that has an old-fashioned type deadbolt that you turn from the inside to lock it. Well, she was able to unlock it, but it wouldn't budge. Then, when she stepped back away from it, she said a face showed up in the bathroom mirror—it was only there a second or two, but it was enough for her. She started screaming and yanking at the door, but it still wouldn't budge. By then, I was finished downstairs and I could hear her hollering and screaming bloody murder. I ran to the bathroom and when I grabbed the door handle, the door just swung open, easy as pie.

Mark tells me it wasn't a pretty sight when his mom came flying out of that bathroom. In fact, it took several minutes to calm her down and hear her story. That's when he and Ginger decided that confession could be good for everyone's soul, and they let mom in on their little secret—that they, too, had come face to face with faces. Surprisingly, upon hearing their tales, Mark's mother slowly became more fascinated than frightened, and admonished them for not letting her know ahead of time what she could run into while visiting there. Then she insisted on looking into every nook and cranny of the house for signs of unearthly residents. "She even wanted us to put a tape recorder in the bathroom," says Mark. "But we sort of resisted that idea. I mean, who really wants to record everything that goes on in the bathroom?" Hmmm. Mark has a point there.

The suggested psychic was telephoned a day or so after Mom's stare-down with the spectral entity of the upstairs commode. She visited the home about a week later, taking time to tour the residence under her conditions—absolute silence. "She didn't want to know any-

thing about the house or what we had run into," says
Ginger. "We just told her we thought we had some
ghosts in the house, that's all."

Upon completion of her tour of duty, the psychic lady
asked if they could talk over a cup of coffee. Obliging
hosts that they are, the three of them sipped cups of
brew and munched from a bag of Oreos as the story of
the haunting spilled forth. "She told us there were at
least two spirits in the house," says Ginger.

> She doesn't call them ghosts, as she says that's deni-
> grating to them. Spirits, she says, are what remains of
> we humans after death. She says these spirits hang
> around because they have unfinished business to take
> care of, or because they really are attached to a
> particular place and don't want to leave it. In our case,
> she said we had a man and a woman, most likely
> husband and wife, who were still hanging around the
> house they had once either owned or lived in. She said
> she had no idea why they chose to show up in our
> mirrors, but that they were really harmless. Well,
> harmless or not, I asked her to make them go away.

Upon receiving said request, the woman insisted on
a few minutes of silence so she could communicate with
the spirits of the couple. Opening her eyes and reaching
for another cookie, she simply announced that the
spirits were now leaving. When asked how she determined this, she replied in a matter-of-fact manner,
"Because I told them they had to go."

The "cleansing" of the spirits from the home was,
perhaps surprisingly, successful, but not until after one
more tête-à-tête. "That night after the psychic left," says
Ginger,

> we went to bed around 11:30. We hadn't been in bed
> long when all of a sudden it was like a heavy breeze
> blew into the bedroom. The lights were out, but we
> both saw this sort of flourescent glow. Pretty soon the
> glowing started spinning around slowly and coming
> closer to the bed. We just lay there while this swirling

mass of light moved around up by the ceiling. Then it seemed to just evaporate.

Terrified once again by the spirits within their home, Mark immediately picked up the phone and used his dial-a-psychic number. "I didn't care what time of night it was," says Mark.

I got that lady out of bed and told her what was going on. I was really pretty upset and mad at this lady for leading us to believe it was all over. She just told me to stay calm, that what we saw was just the spirits of the man and woman leaving the house. She said it was like they had to take one last look around before going. I was still ticked off when I hung up, but you know, we really haven't had any trouble since.

The haunting of Mark and Ginger's home has mercifully abated. Once again they can gaze lovingly into their mirrors and admire one another's features. They feel great relief that all is well now. But what about this author? Over forty years have passed since old Boris scared the slippery snot out of me, and just about the time I started to give nary a thought to spectral images reflecting back at me, I encounter a haunting like this one. No fair. Geez, I hate mirrors.

15

Not This House,
Thank You

Location of Haunting: A large home, well over one hundred years old, in the upscale community of Milford, in Oakland County.

Period of Haunting: This incident reportedly took place in the early 1960s, but hey, with a haunting this strange, it quite possibly continues. At least the experience of the polite folks involved was so intense they have informed me they still aren't sure they'd ever check the place out again.

Date of Investigation: No formal visitation has been made by this ghost lover, although I have twice driven past the residence while in the area. That's the best I could do, since it simply isn't good manners to interrupt the sanctity of a stranger's home with the announcement that their abode is possessed by . . . well, something, and that you'd like to expose it to the world.

Description of Location: Milford must be an attractive settlement for those who enjoy spectral appearances, as this high-rent district also appeared in my first *Haunted Michigan* book. For reasons of propriety, I withhold the address and detailed description of the home in question, although some deft readers may surmise its location from the clues within this text. Suffice it to say that it is on one of the main streets, only a couple blocks from where a thriving real estate agency once existed during the time in question. Oh, what the heck, the place is on Commerce Road, just a few blocks west of Main Street, and not far from a Victorian home currently being occupied by a beauty salon, which has also been the target of ghostly rumors. The home in question looks neither very ancient nor very haunted. So there, torture me if you wish, but that's as close a description as you'll get out of me! In fact, the kind lady who supplied this tale was reluctant to give me the street address because, as she put it, "I don't *want* to remember." To reach the general area, travel M-59 to Milford Road and head south. This route will take you right into town, and from there you should have no real trouble getting a general idea where this place is located. While in town, make it a point to visit the many specialty shops and quaint eateries that comprise the old business district—a fast food sort of town this ain't, and that's good.

The Haunt Meter: * * *

Grace and Joe now reside in Florida, but the experience of that summer's day of long ago is still etched into their minds. Grace insists she has total recall of what happened, in spite of trying for years to forget.

> In the early sixties, my husband, Joe, and I decided we needed a larger house for our rapidly growing family. Thinking to move closer to our friends in Oakland County, we contacted a prosperous real estate agency in the little town of Milford and told them we were interested in any house under $10,000 (author's note: yes, you actually *could* buy a home back then for that amount), over one hundred years old, and with at least three bedrooms and a large yard.

Since Grace and Joe lived almost an hour away from Milford, they had made arrangements for the real estate agency to have their agent contact them if any house even slightly fitting that description should turn up on the market. If the house sounded good, then the two of them would drive up for a look-see whenever Joe got home from work. Thus it was, as Grace puts it, that after one of those telephone calls "we found ourselves in a terrible place one afternoon forty years ago."

Grace and Joe introduced themselves to the agent they had never met before. He came with impeccable references as he worked for the Clay Stokes Agency, a reputable firm now long-since removed from the scene. The agent reported that the home he wanted to show them had just come on the market and that he hadn't had the opportunity to see it yet for himself. That being said, he then drove them the few short blocks to the site. Nothing about the trip there relayed to them any warning of what they were about to experience.

The agent slid his car up against the curb and ushered his clients up the steps and toward the front door. At first glance, everything seemed quite ordinary. They knew the electricity had been disconnected, but it was still light enough outside to make out where things were, and Joe had also thought to bring along a flashlight. The agent unlocked the door, and took about five short steps into the living room, stopping so abruptly that a chain reaction took place with Grace bumping into his backside and Joe bumping into hers. It would have been funny, I guess, if not for the reason everything came to a halt.

"Even forty years later," says Grace,

I can remember clearly the feeling of monstrous evil that enveloped me. It was literally stifling, the air was thick with it. It was as if I had walked into a room full of cotton. There was no actual odor, no drop in temperature, or anything else associated with what you would normally call a "haunting." Just the overwhelming knowledge that I stood in the presence of unimaginable evil—psychotic, perhaps even satanic, evil.

After what seemed like an extended silence, Joe finally asked, "What's the rest of the place like?" and the agent only replied that he had no idea, never offering to give them a guided tour. Joe, obviously the hard-to-intimidate one of the lot, stepped around Grace and the agent, heading off to the left with flashlight in hand. Suddenly not so enthused about gaining a sales commission, the agent opted to keep Grace company near the front door, as neither of them felt any immediate or urgent need for further exploration. After a short while, Joe returned, flashlight in hand, and simply walked out of the house, never uttering a word. The agent turned to lock the door and then announced, "I don't know about you folks, but I think I need a drink."

All the way to the neighborhood tavern, not a word was shared among the auto's three occupants. "We sat in a musty little booth," says Grace,

> and all three of us ordered a beer. I remember making rings on the table with my bottle while the guys talked sporadically about baseball, but mostly we were just quiet, and after one drink we all went home. Never at any time did we three talk about the piece of property we had just seen.

The agent, whose job it is to sell real estate, never even mentioned the selling price. He let his prospective buyers slip out into the darkness without making any attempt to sell them that house. "He never said a word," relates Grace.

> Through the years I have thought that this strange lack of salesmanship was the closest thing I'd ever have to "proof" that whatever crouched in that awful place was felt by all of us. On the way home that night, Joe and I didn't discuss it at all. We were, I think, very busy trying to forget it.

Indeed, Joe and Grace didn't speak of that bizarre night at all for over four years. Then, while camping in Canada with friends, the group began telling the obligatory ghost stories reserved for late-night campfires. With a crackling fire splitting the blackness of night, they listened to first one story and then another. Then Joe, the absolute last person Grace would ever have suspected of joining in on such tomfoolery, began to tell *their* story.

"I was amazed to hear my husband, who was usually skeptical about the paranormal, relating the events of the terrible visit to that awful house to our friends," says Grace.

And it was only then, after four years of silence, that I learned what had happened when he had left me and the real estate agent at the front door and toured the rest of the house alone.

It appeared that to Joe, whoever, or whatever, was causing the ghastly atmosphere in that house either had lived, or was still living, in the back bedroom. As everyone sat in rapt attention around that campfire, he went on to say that everywhere he went in the house left him with a dreaded sense of evil. "Joe said the evil seemed to follow him from room to room," says Grace,

always seeming to be a step or two behind him, a closeness that seemed to make the air too thick to breathe. Then, when he finally reached the back bedroom, he knew that whatever evil thing existed in that home, he had found its place of origin. Several times he tried to enter that room, but didn't, because each time he stepped through the doorway his flashlight went dead. He said that no power on earth could have made him go into that room without a light.

As Grace has told me, there don't seem to be any ghosts in this story, but rather the existence of something intensely evil. Shortly after their camping trip, she and Joe mustered up the courage to re-visit Milford and look the place over once more, from the outside. She says they had a few arguments as to its actual location, but they soon agreed they had found the place. "It was unoccupied," says Grace,

but there appeared to be some remodeling work going

on. I gathered my courage, walked onto the porch, and peered through the living room window. It looked like someone was ripping out all the old lath and plaster and was replacing it with drywall. Perhaps whoever was planning on trying to live there thought it was the prudent thing to do. Can evil *soak* into walls?

Can evil soak into walls? Hmmm. Good question. According to Grace, who still has friends in the Milford area, the house seems to spend a great deal of time on the real estate market. Recently, she made what she calls a half-hearted attempt to check out the history of the place, but succeeded only in discovering that the nineteenth-century family who built it had a good reputation throughout the community and seemed well liked. She doesn't believe this original family is responsible for the evil incarnate within its walls, but then again, she's decided she doesn't really want to know any more about the house after all. Referring to herself and her husband, Grace says, "Neither of us ever have any desire to enter that awful place again."

16

Eugene

Location of Haunting: A private residence in the town of Otsego, in Allegan County, Michigan. The owners of the home prefer the exact address not be published. The author cautions all readers against using their creative energies to locate the home, in the conviction that when privacy is requested, that request needs to be honored.

Period of Haunting: As near as I can tell, this has been a singular experience, rather short in duration. It occurred within the last three years and is included within these pages because I am touched by its gentle, indeed poignant, nature.

Date of Investigation: My first contact with this tale came by means of an e-mail dated January 23, 2001. Subsequent e-mails and phone calls followed, culminating in a final telephone interview on April 9, 2002.

Description of Location: Otsego is a rather small community of about 4,000 souls, just north of Kalamazoo, in extreme southwestern Michigan. One of the many routes leading to the area follows I-94 west to US-131 North. A fifteen-minute drive will take you to Route 89, where you will exit and head west. Otsego is a very brief distance down the road.

The Haunt Meter: * *
While the Haunt Meter gives this story only two stars, don't be misled into thinking this is not a valid, and for that matter, fascinating tale. Remember, the Haunt Meter scale goes up as the story gets more frightening, and this is not a frightening encounter. It is, as I stated earlier, a

warmhearted, touching experience, dear to the hearts of those involved.

Lori and Michael Hudon were united in marriage several years ago and set up housekeeping in Otsego, Lori working as a librarian for the Martin High School, and Michael continuing with his career as a registered nurse. Both their professions and their respectability within the community add credence to this strange story.

Michael brought to the relationship his cats, Eugene and Andy. While they had originally been Michael's feline companions, adding a certain camaraderie into his single life, they quickly became enamored of Lori, accepting her as a pleasant and loving addition to their family. (Bear in mind, we don't own cats, they own us.) While both cats were objects of affection for the Hudons, this particular tale deals with Eugene, the elder pet.

Eugene was given to Michael as a kitten by a friend over twenty years ago and was already nine years old when he and Lori were married. As all cats do, Eugene had his own peculiarities. He loved to lie on the arm of the couch, front legs straddled and head flat, for his numerous daytime naps. He was also wild about cheese, insistent upon snacking on it as often as he could persuade his captive hosts to provide it. And for entertainment, Michael and Lori would wad up a piece of paper into a crumpled ball and play fetch with him. Eugene would stand in a crouched position, muscles tensed and senses heightened, until the paper ball was tossed. Then, in a flash of flying fur, he would pounce on that makeshift ball, pick it up with is teeth, and return it from whence it came, there to await another toss. (Eugene's affinity for cheese and "fetch" makes this author wonder if, as a kitten, his first playmates were dogs and mice.)

Eventually, the years slipped by and Eugene became old and his health began to fail. Experiencing loss of bladder control, he was taken to the vet and diagnosed with kidney failure. Clearly, Eugene was not long for this world. Soon, he was simply lying around the house, sleeping quite often and becoming more and more lethargic as he would seek out places to be alone. Loving him as deeply as they did, this became a giant tug on the heartstrings of both Michael and Lori.

Eventually, Eugene went back to the vet, who decided to perform surgery to see if he could be given a bit more precious time. Surgery only confirmed the worst, however, and Eugene was sent home, where Michael and Lori made his final weeks as comfortable and peaceful as possible.

Eugene sought out a spot to be alone in his last days. He staked out a claim on the basement floor, just under one of the basement lights. For two weeks he could be found there, sleeping and awaiting his passing, coming upstairs only when Michael would seek him out,

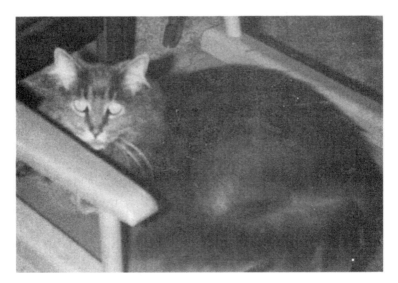

Eugene, the cat, in his director's chair.

carefully enfold him in his arms, and bring him upstairs, where he and Lori could caress his fur and let
him hear their tender voices. Then, Michael would
gingerly return him to his resting place on the basement
floor, under the light.

Lori was quite saddened by Eugene's imminent
demise. As a registered nurse, Michael had encountered
death many times and was perhaps a bit more stoic.
However, Lori recalls one night when her husband
exposed the woundedness of his heart. "We were in bed
for the night," says Lori,

> and Eugene was down in the basement sleeping under
> the light. We were pretty sad about his condition,
> because he really was a part of our family. As we
> quietly lay there, we could hear the soft rumbling of a
> train going by in the distance. That's when Michael
> said, "Well, I guess that's Eugene's train." I knew then
> that this was starting to hurt Michael, too.

Soon after that night, in early November, Eugene
died.

Not long after his passing, Lori began to notice
something strange going on in the basement. The light
directly above where Eugene spent his last weeks in
solitude would inexplicably be found burning brightly.
Lori would turn it off, only to come back later and find it
once again aglow. Some mornings, before leaving for
work, she would check to make certain the light was off,
only to find it illuminating Eugene's corner of the basement upon returning for the day. "The bulb is operated
by a pull string," says Lori,

> I thought maybe Michael was turning it on and forget-
> ting to turn it off, even though I know that's not like
> him at all. But he would tell me he had nothing to do
> with it. Besides, there were times I knew it was off, and
> would go out on an errand, only to find the light on
> when I got home. This happened about a dozen times,
> and the only light affected was the one Eugene always
> lay under during those last two weeks he was alive.

The Hudons found it odd that the light was behaving in such a strange manner, but were, at the time, more fascinated than frightened.

> It wasn't until we went on vacation over Thanksgiving that I was convinced something not normal was taking place. We visited relatives in Kentucky for the holiday, and before we left we checked the house to make sure everything was off and secure. Then, when we came back home and pulled into the driveway, we could tell there was a light on in the basement. Sure enough, it was Eugene's light. At that point I was genuinely startled. I remember thinking to myself, "Oh, my gosh, this really happened!"

Soon after the Thanksgiving experience, the light stopped coming on all by itself. Lori is convinced the whole affair was a purposeful sign, but not directly from Eugene. As a devout Christian, she believes God allowed these strange occurrences as a way to let her know that death is not the end of life and that we continue on. This was especially important for Lori, who up until then had been afraid of death.

Eugene's final resting place.

I feel like God used Eugene's death to prepare me for a new understanding of death. I'm much more at peace now than I was before. I'm not saying it was Eugene who was turning on the light, but that God used these incidents to get a message to me.

I like this story. In particular, I like Lori's interpretation of the somewhat bizarre events that had taken place in her basement. I believe God does speak to us in many symbolic ways. And what better way to teach us a gentle lesson about life and love and death, than through the life, love, and death of such a beloved cat as Eugene.

17

Who (or What) Is Causing All Those Lights?

Location of Haunting: Robbins Pond, the site of the strange phenomenon disclosed herein, is located in Michigan's Upper Peninsula, near the quaint, rustic community of Paulding. Although considered extensively remote by most people's standards, the drive to Robbins Pond alone is more than rewarding in picturesque and panoramic views. Vast forests of evergreens are cut by clear, flowing rivers and creeks. Indeed, this is a truly pristine area, rife with whitetail deer, bear, and just about any other northern creature you wish (or don't wish) to run across.

If you reside in Michigan's Lower Peninsula, you must first cross the Mackinac Bridge, touted as the longest suspension bridge in the world between spans. Be aware that residents from below the bridge are often referred to as "flatlanders" or "trolls" by the locals, but are treated with the quiet respect one would expect from a breed of people who enjoy living close to nature. At any rate, cross the Mighty Mac and head west on US-2, resisting if you can the casinos of St. Ignace. Continue west through Manistique, where you once again will fight the urge to flip a card or spin a reel at yet another Native American owned casino. Stay on US-2, passing through Gladstone and then Escanaba. If you must stop here, try to avoid still another area casino and instead plop down some cash for some truly remarkable handmade candies at Sayklly's Confectionery, on the north side of US-2 in the mall parking lot. From Escanaba carefully follow US-2 west. Here the highway begins to head north by northwest. Eventually, you will reach Highway 45 at a community named Watersmeet. At this point you are practically on the Wisconsin/Michigan border. Turn right on 45, passing through Watersmeet, avoiding, well, you must have it figured out by now, one more casino. About four to five miles up the road you'll see Robbins Pond Road, also known as Forest Highway 5230. Turn left here and travel about two to three miles to Robbins Pond. Park your car off the side of the gravel road and look to the north. On clear nights, the mystery begins.

There is also an alternative route from the Mackinac Bridge, offering a few wonderful views of Lake Superior as you journey westward. Take US-2 west from the bridge, until you get to 77, and turn north. Follow this to US-28, and head west into Munising, the home of Pictured Rocks National Lakeshore. Pause a few hours to take the boat ride to see these spectacular cliffs. When finished, continue west on US-28. The next city you'll pass through will be Marquette, home of Northern Michigan University and quite a few haunted dwellings (stop in at any of the downtown pubs and eateries and just ask the locals). Leave Marquette and stay west on 28 until you reach 45, then go left (south). Follow 45 until you reach—are you ready for this?—Sleepy Hollow Road and turn right. About a mile down this road is Forest Highway 5230, where you'll turn left again. About a mile down the gravel road is Robbins Pond and the infamous mystery lights.

Period of Haunting: Who knows? No one seems to be able to accurately pin a date on just when these strange lights began appearing. Most folks can't recall when they weren't a part of the nightlife around Paulding. Some insist they have relatives who witnessed the lights as far back as the late 1890s, when a locomotive regularly passed through the area with loads of lumber or iron ore. What folks do agree upon is that the haunting continues and can be witnessed on every clear night.

Date of Investigation: Summer of 2002.

Description of Location: Remote. Distant. A place Hemingway would most likely have drooled over. Trout streams and waterfalls. Evergreens and trophy bucks. Northern Lights and lake breezes. Need I continue? For the outdoorsperson, this is a veritable paradise. Located just south of the Keweenaw Peninsula and the Porcupine Mountains, most of the locals agree that God's area code is undoubtedly 906.

The Haunt Meter: * *

Not scary, but intriguing . . .

A good many stories have been written about the lights of Paulding. Just go online with such search words as "Paulding" or "ghost lights," and you're likely to find several sites housing copious amounts of information and speculation on their origins and legends. And while I have always made it a point not to write about any ghost, haunting, or paranormal event already in print, I make the exception here. My reason for so doing is the simple fact that my eldest son, Rob, a high school teacher, guidance counselor, and sex abuse counselor, has experienced the strange ghostly lights up front and personally. When a person of his integrity stands amazed at what he encountered, I take the tale seriously.

This is, indeed, a well-documented paranormal phenomenon. The Marquette, Michigan, television station has filmed the lights, and several newspapers and magazines have done likewise. Photographs abound, showing forth the mysterious balls and streaks of light, sometimes green, sometimes red, often white, scooting across the clear northern skies. Hundreds of people speak openly of their experiences with the lights, and unashamedly so. The origin and nature of these lights have been so baffling for so many decades that even *Ripley's Believe It or Not* at one time offered $100,000 to anyone who could prove what they were. Although no professional explanation has been proffered, Ripley's has since rescinded the reward.

My son, Rob, encountered the lights quite by accident. He and his significant other, Tracy, were visiting the community of Watersmeet, where both were considering teaching positions. They had spent the day in interviews and passed away the late afternoon and evening looking for adequate housing. Tired and ready for a good night's rest, they pulled in to the parking lot of their hotel quite late and began to retrieve their luggage from the trunk of the car. "I happened to glance up at the night sky," says Rob,

> which is always so clear and beautiful, when I saw a streak of light go flashing across the sky, headed northward. I know it wasn't a shooting star, because it was far too brilliant and obvious. I remember I was stunned somewhat, and I asked Tracy if she had seen it. She said that she had and wondered what it could have been. At that point we didn't know anything at all about the lights of Paulding out by Robbins Pond, so we just went to our room and straight to bed. The next day, while checking out the scenery in the countryside, we passed by Robbins Pond and saw the sign the Michigan Forest Service put up about the lights. That's when we realized what we had encountered.

Most paranormal activity is pooh-poohed by any official agency of any given government, so it is with amusement and amazement one finds an official branch of state government endorsing—and even encouraging— the belief in these strange paranormal encounters. I mean, if taxpayer money is used to pay for a sign attesting to these strange events, shouldn't they be taken seriously?

Theories abound as to the nature of these lights. I

refer to them as "ghostly" lights because some of the more prominent theories place their origin in some sort of tragic human event that caused the exit of one mortal and the entry of one ghost. The most widely accepted theory is that these lights are the ghost of a railway conductor, killed one night when he exited the stopped train at Robbins Pond to make some sort of an inspection. It is said the poor, unfortunate man got his signals a bit mixed up, and the train suddenly began moving backward instead of forward, crushing him under its massive wheels. The lights, as those who accept this story are wont to believe, are the glow of his lantern as he makes his nightly inspection of the area, just as he did on that tragic evening over one hundred years ago. No one seems to know why he doesn't just move on to that great railway junction in the sky, but they find it entertaining that he hasn't. Many locals contend there are occasions when you can catch the faint sounds of a locomotive passing by, especially curious because the tracks have been gone from the area for decades.

Another bit of speculation claims the lights are really the ghost of a man killed by a jealous husband. Seems a lumberjack was in love with an engineer's wife, and the engineer looked upon the relationship with a certain amount of disdain. Some men are like that. Anyway, he confronted the lumberjack with a display of animated anger designed to scare the man off the perfume-scented trail of his beloved. It didn't work. The lumberjack dispatched the poor dumb slob on the spot. Even if the engineer did have morality and a justified sense of hostility on his side, you just don't mess with a northern Michigan lumberjack. At any rate, the ghost of the engineer is said to haunt the skies over the area, pining away over the woman he lost. Interesting, but as with the first explanation, there's really nothing in print anywhere to substantiate the story.

The lights themselves are an enigma. Some say they are streaks of light, shooting across the night skies, while others insist they are balls of light, sometimes way off in the distance, and sometimes only a few yards away from the beholder. There isn't even agreement on what color they are. They have been reported as blue, white, red, green, and even purple. Some say they are of mixed colors. Although they are not in agreement as to color, they are in agreement they can be seen nearly every cloudless evening, from late dusk well into the wee hours of the morning.

This author has had several contacts with persons willing to speak of the mystery lights of Robbins Pond. More than one individual asserts they have not only videotaped the lights, but have made audio recordings of voices in the area. One woman, whose name is withheld at request, told me in a telephone conversation that she and her boyfriend parked out on the gravel road by Robbins Pond with the intent of proving for themselves that something strange is going on out there. When she played back her recorder the next day, she picked up a man's voice saying something like, "I'm going now," and a woman's voice whispering, "I'm lonely."

This same informant tells me that many in the area believe the spot around the pond is a portal for souls to cross over from this world to the next. She even maintains that the local Native Americans adhere to this belief. If so, it would seem to be a great place to take photographs, videotape, and audio recordings. The only difficulty would be finding a nice clear night when not many people are parked alongside the road, hoping for a personal encounter of their own. It is a popular spot for ghost watching.

I find it interesting that these lights are seen so often—every clear night according to the locals. I also find it intriguing that the path of their flight follows the power line right-of-way. One cannot help but wonder if there is some sort of connection here, yet folks up there are insistent that's all been checked out and disproved.

I've not heard of any professional paranormal investigators staking the place out. I don't recall having heard of any psychics doing their thing out there either. If a serious study of the phenomenon is ever undertaken, I'd be anxious to peruse their results. In the meantime, you can check out the place for yourself. If you don't have any luck there, you can always check out one of the nearby casinos. There's a few flashing lights in them, too.

18

Just Who Is This Woman, Anyway?

Location of Haunting: Westland, Michigan, is a rambling suburb of Detroit in southeastern Michigan. It is bordered by Wayne, Livonia, and Inkster, to name a few.

Period of Haunting: Unknown. The ghost in this yarn is affectionately known as "Grandma," not only by the current residents who contacted me, but by some of the neighbors as well. The neighbors claim the haunting goes back several years, but cannot pinpoint when it began or just who "Grandma" could have been.

Date of Investigation: Spring of 2002.

Description of Location: The home in question is a wood-frame, single-family residence on a quiet street named Creston. It was built sometime in the early 1960s, which means our ghost has been haunting this happy abode for somewhere between twenty-five and forty years. Since the current residents of the home would rather not entertain people they don't know—with the exception of their ghost, of course—they have asked that their names and the exact location of their home be kept confidential.

The Haunt Meter: * * *

Dutch and Sandi Holcomb noticed something was a bit amiss shortly after they moved into their new home on Creston Avenue. It wasn't anything overt that caught their interest, but small, almost unnoticeable things. When activity began to escalate over the years, they naturally became more and more concerned. They weren't worried about their safety, or that of their children, but were deeply puzzled about what they had begun to witness and experience. They had a copy of my last book and after a bit of simple research contacted me. As is usual in such situations, I converse first by e-mail and then by phone if I feel at ease doing so. I soon became quite comfortable with the Holcombs and agreed to check out the house and listen to their story.

Dutch and Sandi turned out to be charming hosts, offering coffee and cinnamon bread around the kitchen table as we dispensed with the obligatory small talk. Having deposited a few degrees of initial nervousness in the recycling bin, they got right down to the subject of the visit. "We started noticing small things right away," said Sandi, self-consciously stirring her coffee.

> I'd go downstairs for something and when I'd come back up, if I left a kitchen light on, it would be off. Or, sometimes when I'd be cooking breakfast or supper, if I'd go outside, like to get the mail or something, when I'd go back in the kitchen the stove would be off. At first I just dismissed it as stuff I must have done myself and forgot about, but then I started paying more attention, and pretty soon I knew it wasn't me that was doing it.

The Holcombs continued their strange tale, consisting of the usual sort of parapsychological phenomena— lights switching on or off, doors being opened or closed, the sounds of things being moved when no one is near. The difference here, though, was that there seemed to be a purpose rather than a pattern to it all.

"Everything seemed, how can I say it, like someone or something was being overly cautious," says Sandi.

> Like the plants I keep by the front window. Every morning I open the drapes so they can get sun. A

couple of times I guess I was late getting the drapes opened up because I'd go in to do it, and they'd already be open. It was like I was getting help keeping my plants healthy. But I'd really rather not have the help.

Sandi is not the only member of the family to get a helping unseen hand around the house. Sometimes Dutch is the recipient of otherworldly benevolence. "I will never forget the time Sandi was fixing supper and had to run next door for a minute to the neighbor's house for some reason," he says.

She asked me to put the crescent rolls in the oven and listen for the timer when they were done. She was really emphatic about my not burning them, because there's a standing joke in our family that anytime I'm put in charge of anything cooking in the kitchen, I reduce it all to ashes. I guess I'm sort of brain dead when it comes to cooking. Anyway, I put the rolls in the oven and got busy with some project down in the basement. All of a sudden I remembered those rolls, and man, this was like way past the time they were supposed to come out. Just as I was going up the stairs, I heard Sandi come home. She was already in the kitchen when I got upstairs, and she said something like, "I don't believe it, you remembered the rolls." Sure enough, they were out of the oven and cooling on top of the stove. I didn't say anything about it until after we ate. Then we both got really good and freaked out.

It's not that Dutch and Sandi don't appreciate the help around the old homestead, it's just that they aren't comfortable with an unseen houseguest wandering around at will, picking up after them. "I'm just so afraid," says Sandi,

that I'm going to turn around some day and see it. I don't want to see whoever it is. So far, I can stand the strange stuff to a degree, but if I ever see who's doing all this stuff, well, I know that if Eloise was still open that's where I'd end up.

(For those not in the know, Eloise was a sprawling

complex of ominous structures connected by underground tunnels and surrounded by high fences, housing a state-operated mental institution until it was razed
several years back. A Kroger store now occupies much
of the area, and some folks claim it has inherited the
ghosts of some of the patients who passed through—
and away—there.)

The coffee was good, the cinnamon bread better, and
the conversation even more delightful. As I took notes,
I'd frequently use a pause in the conversation to ask a
question or two. One of them dealt with whether or not
they had any idea who was haunting their home. "It's a
woman," said Dutch.

> We kind of figured that out by the nature of what was
> happening, but we found out for sure a few weeks ago.
> A buddy of mine from work asked if he could drop by
> and borrow my wheelbarrow. I told him we wouldn't be
> home that evening, but that I'd leave the side door of
> the garage unlocked for him and he could help himself.
> I only asked that he lock the door when he was
> finished. Well, he came over while we were gone, and
> got what he needed out of the garage. But he said that
> when he came out of the garage he could see an old
> woman watching him from the back bedroom window.
> He said he waved and smiled at her, but she just
> turned away. He said he took the wheelbarrow out to
> the curb and loaded it in his pickup, and then went
> back to turn out the light in the garage and lock the
> door up. When he got to the garage, he said the light
> was already out and the door was locked. He figured it
> was the old woman, and that she must have been one
> of our grandmothers. I told him it was because I really
> didn't want anyone knowing we had a ghost in the
> house. But that's how we finally found out for sure
> that it was a woman doing all this stuff.

I also asked if they had psychics or organized ghosthunters over to check out the place, and they said they
hadn't. Then they asked if I could recommend any
trustworthy organizations in the area, and I politely

informed them that I hesitate to make such referrals.

With the Holcombs's permission I took a few photographs of the inside of the house, but assured them I wouldn't use any photos of the outside, as they wanted privacy. My hope, as with all photos I take, was to pick up something on film. But, as is usually the case, the photographs turned out perfectly normal.

An interesting sidelight to this story is that it is in my book at all. I almost *never* do a chapter where so few witnesses are available to substantiate the story. Why, then, did I include their tale? First, the Holcombs wanted no publicity of any kind—that was their prerequisite to our meeting. Secondly, they had nothing to gain by letting me use their story for my book. And lastly, they were interested in further help only if a professional, organized team from a respected university was involved. Even then, they didn't believe their own haunting to merit such attention.

Originally, this chapter was supposed to end about here. However, just about the time I was putting the finishing touches on this book, the Holcombs contacted me once again. It seems their ghost was getting a bit bolder as of late. "We were in bed one night last week," says Sandi,

and I sort of drifted awake. That's something that I almost never do, and I was a little curious about it. Then I heard what sounded like humming coming from out in the living room. It sounded like a woman humming. I woke up Dutch, and he heard it too. It was like a soft, whispering kind of humming. It didn't scare us; in fact, it sounded soothing. Eventually, it went away and we went back to sleep. It wasn't until morning that we got scared, after we had time to talk about it and think about it.

The haunting of the Holcomb residence isn't a particularly frightening one. Obviously, someone's grandmother seems to be attached to the home for some reason. Sandi and Dutch insist it can't be any of their relatives, since three out of four of their grandmothers are still living, and the deceased grandmother has been dead for some thirty-five years and has never visited anyone yet. I guess sometimes we just have no idea what criteria ghosts use to pick the places and people they intend to visit. And I'm not John Edwards, so don't ask me.

19

A Haunted Dwelling in the Author's Birthplace!

Location of Haunting: A rambling old house, built pre-Civil War, in the blue-collar town of Ypsilanti, Michigan, skirting the town of Ann Arbor.

Period of Haunting: The family involved in this haunting lived in the home in question for a few years before moving to Leslie, Michigan, about six years ago. That makes this haunting relatively recent. Considering the nature of the haunting and the fact that the family doesn't seem to be bothered in their new abode, reason would dictate that the haunting preceded them and most likely continues to impress the fortunate inhabitants who currently call the place home.

Date of Investigation: This story was first related to me in January of 2001. This is not a place I have personally visited, but judging from the nature of the haunting and my familiarity with how many homes in Ypsilanti are currently experiencing ghostly activity, I include it within these pages.

Description of Location: Ypsilanti is a mostly work-a-day sort of city situated about thirty-five miles west of the city of Detroit. It is one of the oldest of Michigan's cities and was one of the first communities settled as a result of westward expansion along the Old Sauk Trail, which became US-12, once the major artery between Detroit and Chicago. The historic district boasts a number of Victorian-style homes, many of which have been converted into apartment houses to glean rental cash from students at nearby Eastern Michigan University. The university was once called Michigan Normal School, where, years ago, most Michigan teachers received their training. The address of the home is not offered, as the former residents don't wish recriminations from current residents if they don't take well to the public knowledge that their house is haunted. Incidentally, Ypsilanti now runs fluidly into Ann Arbor, home to the University of Michigan. Both cities offer some wonderful dining establishments, especially in downtown Ann Arbor, where many restaurants offer outdoor seating and terrific Middle Eastern cuisine. Of course, Ypsilanti retaliates with Depot Town, the northeastern part of the city where the trains still run through. There are too many great eateries in that area to list, so I'll not recommend one. I'll just let you know that when President Clinton was in town, he dined at one of the restaurants in Depot Town.

The Haunt Meter: * * ½

Susan is an active, imaginative young woman who now resides in Leslie, Michigan, which is itself a very haunted community. However, Susan's haunting experiences are not associated with her hometown, but with a home she and her family occupied some six years ago in Ypsilanti. Susan, married a dozen years and mother of three, says she has always been "into" the spirit world—hauntings in particular—and is fascinated with the interaction between apparitions and those of us who still inhabit this mundane physical world.

"The house we rented," says Susan,

> was built in the pre-Civil War era. As soon as we moved in I began to realize I was always cold, but my husband pooh-poohed it all by saying it was just an old, drafty house.

Drafty may be one explanation for damp, clammy feelings, but it is clearly not the explanation that suited

Susan—especially when she and her younger daughter began to share encounters that defied rational explanation. "One day," she says,

> when my seven-year-old daughter was only one year old, I had placed her in her walker and gave her free run of the living room so she could play while I got some housework taken care of. After a few minutes had passed, I realized I could hear her laughing and laughing, you know, the way a child does when someone is entertaining them. I thought I'd peek in to see what was so entertaining to her, and when I went into the room to see what she was up to, she was staring at the fireplace, laughing away, just like she would do when someone would make faces for her. I stood in the doorway for a minute and watched, and she kept looking at the direction of the fireplace, very amused.

Susan found herself intrigued by her daughter's behavior, because she was making no attempt to take the free run of the living room she had been given, but was instead totally engrossed in whoever was between her walker and the fireplace. "Finally," says Susan,

> I stepped all the way into the living room and approached her walker. When she heard me coming, she spun around toward me, then immediately spun back toward the fireplace. When she did, she said, "Bye-bye," at whoever she was playing with, and then turned around and started walking over to me. I really didn't feel anything strange about what I saw, even though I knew there had to be someone in there she was looking at. Since whoever it was had been taking time to play with a little girl, I figured it couldn't be anyone with bad intentions, so I just let it be. I didn't even mention it to my husband when he came home from work.

It appears that dear old hubby would soon be informed of the strange goings-on in the creaky old house, as the otherworld activity began to escalate just a tad. Not long after the incident with her daughter, Susan was once again toiling away in the kitchen. She happened to be alone in the kitchen that afternoon, with the living room stereo tuned to one of her favorite radio stations. "The station the radio was on kept going in and out," says Susan,

> and then all of a sudden it went to all static. I thought it was odd, because I'd listen to that station a lot during the day and it would never give me any trouble. It was a local station, so the signal was always strong, but all of a sudden, there was the static.

Susan decided to check out what was up with the stereo and walked into the living room to fix the problem. "When I walked into the living room," she says,

> a heavy candle holder that I always kept on the fireplace mantle just fell off onto the floor and rolled about two feet. At the same time, the radio station I was listening to came back in as strong as ever, all by itself.

Again, Susan says she didn't sense anything frightening, even though she knew she was in the presence of someone who was obviously trying to catch her attention. "I didn't have any fear or anything like that," she says,

> and I just said hello to whoever it was and told them that they were welcome to be there with me that day, but to please not knock my things over to get my attention. Then I thanked them, picked up the candleholder, and put it back where it belonged. Then I went back to my housework.

When Susan's husband came home from work, she filled him in on the strange events of the afternoon, but, as usual, he scoffed at the very idea of ethereal guests playing shenanigans with the decor. He assured her there was always a rational explanation for such things and insisted she must have set the candleholder too close to the edge of the mantle and it slipped off and onto the floor. "I knew there was no way it fell off by itself," says Susan, so I led my husband into the living room and showed him where I had always kept the candleholder, well away from the edge of the mantle. That candleholder is at least six inches long and made of heavy brass. It has a large, squared bottom, and can't just vibrate off the mantle all by itself, especially since my other knick-knacks hadn't moved a smidgen. Then I asked him to try to roll that heavy squared holder across the floor, which he couldn't do. I think that's when he began to believe something just might be going on around that old house.

Throughout their tenure within those mysterious walls, paranormal activity continued on a fairly regular basis. Never were Susan or any of her children ever blatantly frightened by the spirits who seemed to be working hard to get their attention. Instead, they were somewhat intrigued. "Nothing was ever scary to us," says Susan.

But strange stuff was always going on. For instance, our dog, who loved to play with the kids, began to play with someone who wasn't there, at least, someone none of us could ever see. You'd swear that crazy dog was playing fetch, you know, standing in one area of the living room wagging its tail, and then suddenly running off like it was chasing something, and then running back to where it started from. It kept running back and forth like this for several minutes, until I guess the ghost got tired of playing and went away.

It is said that animals are good indicators of whether or not a home is haunted. More than one person I've interviewed over the years has reported strange pet habits such as this, and even Karliss Osis, the former head of the American Society for Psychical Research, a prestigious organization dedicated to the scientific investigation of paranormal activity, once told me to watch the cats and dogs in houses purported to be haunted, that they will often let you know when the ghosts are moving about. This is true of a housecat I came to know who resided in a *very* haunted house in Wooster, Ohio.

I had spent dozens of days in that odd house, experiencing more spectral shivers than I had bargained for. Invariably, the ghostly activity was preceded by that infuriated feline hissing and snapping at someone over in the corner of the living room that I couldn't see, but certainly could sense.

Susan says the ghost, or ghosts, in her Ypsilanti home soon decided her husband needed a nocturnal nudge to make a confirmed believer out of him. Over a period of several nights, he would awaken to hear the sound of footsteps trudging around upstairs when everyone was supposed to be neatly tucked away for the night. He would awaken his wife, and the two of them would listen to plodding footsteps much too heavy to belong to any of their children. Many were the nights he would exit the comfort of his warm bed to explore the rooms above him, only to find that the footsteps would cease the moment he reached the top of the stairs. Upon inspection, all of the kids would be found snuggled up nice and warm in their respective beds. "He was fooled like this night after night," says Susan, "until he had to admit he couldn't explain what was going on up there and admitted that just maybe we did have a ghost or two wandering around the house."

Eventually, the time came for Susan and her family to move back to Leslie, the lovely mid-Michigan town where she was born and raised. However it wasn't the ghosts who convinced them to move, the mundane reason being no more frightening than a simple job transfer. "The night before we moved," recalls Susan,

> I stayed up really late to finish up some packing. I was in the kitchen, sealing up boxes, and out of the corner of my eye I saw something move toward the stairs. At first I thought it was one of my boys who had gotten out of bed, so I walked on over to see what was up, but there wasn't anyone there. So I went to check on the boys and they were asleep in their beds. So, I figured it must be my friend from beyond. For the next half hour

or so, as I finished packing up the kitchen, I talked to that person. As I talked, I thanked that person (Susan uses the term "person" because she was never certain whether her houseguest was male or female) for sharing their home with us for the past three years. I also said thanks for being so kind to my daughter, because there were many nights when she would cry, but by the time I would get to her room, the ghost would already have been there and turned her crying into giggles. As I spoke, I turned around and saw a faint, white image standing in the hall. I could make out a young woman's face, and I got the sense that she was very touched by my appreciation. It was the first time I realized our ghost was female. She was only visible for a moment or two, and then she vanished.

Susan says that the encounter with her female specter that last night in the house was so touching she had to stop what she was doing and sit down for a moment.

I could actually sense this young woman saying "thank you" to me. Leaving that place was actually sort of sad, even though I was going back to my hometown. To this day, my kids still ask me to tell them the story of what happened that night. They never get tired of hearing about our ghost in Ypsi. My husband, however, just laughs. I think he's back to not wanting to believe anything strange was going on there.

Throughout my visits to dozens of haunted dwellings, both private and public, I've been intrigued by the fact that many people consider their ghosts to be helpful, even watchful, caring for the house and the occupants. The impression I get is that ghosts sometimes enjoy sharing close quarters with those of us limited to this physical plane of ours. At any rate, more than one homeowner has assured me that, given the choice, they would much rather abide with their sprits than without them.

Beyond
the State Line

*Did the author unknowingly capture a ghost in this
vacation photo from Gettysburg Battlefield?
Read "Who Is That Woman in the Photograph?"*

20

Who Is That Woman in the Photograph?

Authors Note: Although the intent of this book is to address Michigan haunted places, the following descriptions of roosts for the dead in other states have been included as a sidelight. I thought you'd enjoy hearing about them.

Location of Haunting: The Gettysburg Battlefield, a National Historic Site in Gettysburg, Pennsylvania, just north of the Maryland state line.

Period of Haunting: According to folklorists, National Park Service personnel, parapsychologists, and scores of visitors over many decades, it appears this battlefield, scene of some of the fiercest fighting of the Civil War, has been haunted since the bloody battle itself.

Date of Investigation: Actually, this story does not recount an official investigation of any sort, but is a more personal tale, the telling of a ghostly encounter that took place in the scorching hot Pennsylvania summer of 1997.

Description of Location: If anyone reading this account is unfamiliar with the Gettysburg Battlefield, or even its location, I admonish you for not having listened more attentively to the history instructors of your youth. Still, if you must be told, Gettysburg is a charming small town tucked away among the quiet hills of southern Pennsylvania. The residents make every attempt to keep alive the memories of the battle that ravaged their town and countryside over those three terrible days in July, 1863. Visiting Gettysburg is tantamount to visually, if not physically, going back in time. The main street is lined with period homes, many of which literally extend to the curb. Gettysburg truly seems to transport the visitor to the nineteenth century, and residents openly exert their energies to keep it that way. Shops, restaurants, and lodging facilities explode with tourist paraphernalia, all geared toward whetting the appetites of history buffs—and in particular, Civil War buffs—everywhere.

As far as haunting events are concerned, the town of Gettysburg has been in the public eye for decades. National television programs have focused their cameras on this quaint town on many occasions, recounting terrifying tales of face-to-face encounters with ghosts and hoping to videotape any specter polite enough to pose for posterity. As if that weren't enough, scores of books have been penned about apparitions floating around practically everywhere, from the battlefield to the bed-and-breakfasts, and even in the backs of pickup trucks (a strange means of transportation for an apparition, but everybody has their favorite mode of coming and going). Virtually every gift shop in town sells the books, and there are even "ghost tours" available for those who wish to visit the rumored haunted sites that mark the region. These hauntings are so widely accepted by the locals, that there is no effort whatsoever to hush them. In fact, if you were to phone the local Chamber of Commerce and make inquiries into the coziest haunted hotel in the area, the cordial folks there would cheerfully direct you to your pick of several—most offering warm beds, country breakfasts, and the distinct possibility of snuggling in for the night with a vaporous, non-paying guest.

It is believed that the town of Gettysburg is so heavily haunted because of the famous battle that took place within its streets and all around the adjoining countryside. The rebel forces of such Confederate giants as Lee, Longstreet, and Pickett exchanged muzzle volleys, cannon shot, and infantry attack with the Union true blues of Meade, Buford, and Reynolds. When the smoke finally cleared, the landscape was littered with corpses. Tens of thousands of men were killed or wounded in such famous sites as "The Peach Orchard," "Devil's Den," "Little Round Top," and the tragic expanse of open field known today as the site of Pickett's Charge. It is widely accepted that this horrific carnage resulted in all sorts of blue- or grey-clad ghosts, possibly trapped in time by their sudden departures from this earthly plane. If you think the town is haunted, it appears the battlefield dwarfs it in comparison. Photos, videotapes, and tape recordings abound with seeming evidence of the long dead, still roaming through the fields in search of their lost regiments.

The Haunt Meter: * * ½

Because this story isn't really very frightening, it rates a rather mediocre scoring on "The Haunt Meter." However, ghostly encounters do not require ghastly terror to still be considered eerie. Certainly, at least from my perspective, this story is quite strange, perhaps even more so when one considers that I was making no attempt whatsoever to contact any of the spirts haunting this historic site. The subject of ghosts was far removed from my mind.

In late July of 1997, my wife and I invited her parents to join us on a trip to Gettysburg Battlefield. The intent was to quench some of our thirst for first-hand knowledge of the battlefield itself, as we were all interested in American history and, in particular, Civil War history. Ever since I was a child, I had harbored a deep fascination for the Civil War, as many of my toys so aptly reflected—blue kepi, miniature soldiers, toy muzzle-loaders, etc. So it was with some of that youthful fervor propelling me forward that we headed off down the highway toward Pennsylvania, and that tragic site so dear to my childhood dreams.

Having arrived too late in the day to accomplish anything of significance, we caught a hotel room on the outskirts of town. We arose the next morning to a blistering July sun, with the temperature in the high 80s before breakfast. We slid into the car, drove through town, and spent about an hour in the visitor's center picking up a few souvenirs and watching a very helpful video explaining the three-day progress of the battle. Declining a guided tour, we opted for a $9-cassette for the car stereo, a tape designed for those who like to linger in particular areas of the battlefield unencumbered by the dictates of time and park guide.

To say the battlefield and the descriptions of the events of those three days was a powerful experience is an understatement. Our camera shutters clicked incessantly. Around noon, we dined on a picnic luncheon of fried chicken and potato salad at the very location where General Reynolds, astride his horse and encouraging his men, was blasted through the neck by a Confederate sharpshooter. On this day I was anything but a ghost-hunter—I was, embarrassing to admit, the stereotypical tourist, replete with sunglasses, shorts, camera bag, and sunscreen.

By mid-afternoon, we were all beaded with sweat as the thermometer flirted with a temperature somewhere in the range of ninety-five degrees. Because of the sweltering conditions, the park was nearly devoid of other tourists. With the sun urging us to find air-conditioned relief, I decided there was really only one thing left that I really wanted to do. I wanted a photograph of the scene of Pickett's Charge, the highwater mark of the battle for the Confederacy, which ended in the bloody destruction of nearly all of General Pickett's command.

In stark contrast to the carnage of that long-ago day, that particular location is now one of the most beautiful sites in the park. A grove of hardwoods overlooks a vast tract of open field about one-mile deep. In front of that clump of trees sits a beautiful period cannon, still pointing in the direction from whence came the enemy in butternut. I knew immediately that this was the setting for the "perfect" photograph of the day.

Although the four of us were the only ones in that section of the battlefield, I wanted to ensure that nothing or no one would interfere with my efforts for the perfect shot. I assigned each of my in-laws to guard duty on either side of the cannon, but well out of lens view of my camera. My wife staked out the parking lot, ready to toot the horn if any tourists dared invade my territory. Absolutely certain no one was anywhere nearby, I snapped three successive photos of the scene before me. Then, we finished our touring and headed off to dine in the air-conditioned splendor of the nearest café.

The film I shot during that vacation was developed within days of our return to Michigan. Most of the photos were quite typical of those taken by any tourist, so it was with some degree of muted excitement that I searched for my "perfect" photos. When I finally came across them, I was struck by how well they had actually turned out. The cannon, the green stand of hardwoods, the blue sky flecked with wisps of white clouds. But I was also struck by something else. Of the three photos I had taken of that site, one had an added attraction. Standing behind the camera, arms folded and staring back at my lens, was a woman. For the life of me, I couldn't recall anyone being nearby when I took the pictures, and my wife and in-laws assured me that we were indeed alone at the time they were taken.

I thumbed through the negatives until I found the appropriate set, and held them up to the light. I had snapped three pictures of that cannon, yet this woman only showed up on one of the negatives. Furthermore, she was only on the middle negative of the three. Only a matter of seconds had separated those snapshots, and I am certain there was no time for anyone to have entered the area without notice. Intrigued, I retrieved a magnifying glass from my desk and settled in for a closer examination of the mystery before me.

What I viewed under the lens of that glass was absolutely unsettling. The woman in question seems to have stepped into view from another time. Her honey-colored hair is all stacked up on her head in what my wife simply describes as a bun. She is wearing a white blouse with puffy sleeves down to her wrists and a ruffled collar that rises almost to her chin. From her waist to the ground she is adorned with a yellow skirt. No one in their right mind would have worn anything other than shorts and the lightest of clothing on that scorching Pennsylvania afternoon. Yet, there she is, standing in my photograph, arms folded, staring directly into the camera, as solid as you or me.

I include the photograph for your examination (see p. 199). Many who have seen it have asked me if there had been an historical re-enactment of some sort going on in the park that day. There wasn't. Others maintain it was simply some tourist wandering around the cannons and inadvertently ruining my shot. This theory doesn't fly for three reasons: one, everyone in my party swears we were alone at the time the photos were taken; two, there was no way she had "inadvertently" done anything, as she appears to be posing for the photo; and, three, she only appears on the second negative, while the first and third show no trace of her anywhere.

I am always intrigued, and somewhat amused, at photos people show me of their ghosts. Invariably, what you see are smoky mists, streaks or balls of light, or translucent mists resembling double exposures. In this photo, the ghost—and I am convinced it is a ghost—is as

solid and colorful as any physical being. For that matter, the only ghosts I have ever encountered have been
just like her.

So, look for yourself, and make up your own mind. If
you're convinced I'm correct, that's fine. If you think I'm
trying to pull one over on you, so be it. I already have
the only confirmation I need.

21

It's Still Alma's House

Location of Haunting: The Alma Matthews House is located at 275 W. 11th Street, in the Greenwich Village section of New York City.

Period of Haunting: According to their own literature, the place has been haunted for quite some time now, ever since the death of the woman for whom the structure is named, Alma Matthews.

Date of Investigation: Summer of 2000. Follow up, summer of 2001.

Description of Location: The Alma Matthews House is a brownstone structure, four stories high and with a full, if antiquated, basement. It is quite typical of housing in the area, most of which are nineteenth-century row houses. (You know, they're attached to one another.) Greenwich Village is an extraordinary place to visit, if not live. The streets are narrow, parking practically non-existent, trees even more scarce, and actual yards unheard of. Having said all that, I must admit it is one of my all-time favorite places to visit. The eclectic atmosphere is unrivaled. You will see it all in Greenwich Village, even if you don't want to see it all.

To arrive at the address in question, I offer these directions. Fly into LaGuardia Airport, line up at the cabstand out front, and when it comes your turn to slide into the backseat of one of these legendary modes of urban transportation, just offer the driver the address above. It's about a thirty-minute, $25-thrill ride from LaGuardia. I've yet to make the trip without a severe case of motion sickness, for which I am always reluctant to tip the cabbie.

The building itself is somewhat narrow, yet roomy. It served for years as a home for single women trying to make their way in a large city. Alma Matthews owned the place and offered this service, making certain the women were well cared for and safe. She was quite active in her church and saw it as a type of ministry.

I have stayed several times at the Alma Matthews House. The ground floor houses a reception area, elevator, sitting room, and lounge—dry, of course; it's now a United Methodist hotel of sorts where folks associated with the denomination can stay cheaply while visiting the city on business. The floors above are divided into several guest rooms, all rather rustic by today's modern standards, but nonetheless comfortable. There are no televisions, the air-conditioning consists of individual units perched precariously upon windowsills, and until recently, there were no telephones in any of the guest rooms. There are, however, Bibles on every night stand. It's a retreat from the niceties of the rest of the city. I must admit I enjoyed all my stays there, particularly because of its location. Anything you want is not far away, which can be both good and bad.

You can spend a little or a lot here. I prefer a little. On the west end of the block is a fabulously good Chinese restaurant, and other ethnic eateries are liberally sprinkled all over the area. There's a great place to dine on bangers and mash, the Irish grub that washes down well with a pint of Guinness, but I'll not tell you where it is. Part of the fun of Greenwich Village is exploring the area for yourself, finding places to suit your own tastes. As for entertainment, you name it and it's most likely there. I arrived once during the famous Halloween parade and was struck dumb by the (lack of) costumes on display. It's the kind of place where restaurants spill out on to the sidewalks, and the streets are always crowded, any time of day or night. And despite what you've heard, I've never once been frightened for my safety in the village. Even though the Alma Matthews House is a denominational hostelry, it may be possible for you to reserve a room there for your visit, at a greatly reduced rate from what local hotels attempt to suck out of you.

The Haunt Meter: * * * ½

There are times when I seem to unwittingly attract ghosts. I don't know why, but I've been this way for a good part of my life. I can't summon them, they just seem to show up. That's pretty much what happened to me at this location.

My trip had begun innocently enough. I had come to the Big Apple on church business. My paid expenses included a bed at the Alma Matthews House. Having arrived under the influence of motion sickness, I grudgingly tipped my cab driver and stumbled my way up the cement steps and into the reception area. I was given a room on the fourth floor and, not having the stomach for the elevator ride, opted for the stairs.

The room was large, with a single bed and desk. The bath was down the hall to be shared with residents of other rooms. As excited as I was to be in New York for the first time, all I wanted right then was to lie flat on my back and fight off nausea. As I lay there, I kept feeling the mattress depress as though someone was poking it hard with a finger. I know I wasn't imagining it, because my stomach offered confirmation. At that point, I didn't much care if it was elves or Elvis, I just needed to get my balance once again.

After a bit, my stomach settled down and my headache fell to a five on the Richter Scale. Since the room was no longer swimming, I was able to sit up once again. About the time I realized I could actually go out and get something to eat, I felt the mattress suddenly sag a bit once more. It's funny how, if you think you're dying, you don't much care if there are ghosts in the room with you, but when you're feeling up to par it matters more than a little. I left the bed for the comfort of the armchair by the desk and kept watch of the mattress. Nothing unusual happened for several minutes, and just about the time I thought I would go downstairs, a sudden cold draft wafted past me. It was quite noticeable since the day was unearthly hot and I hadn't yet turned on the air conditioner.

I headed downstairs and struck up a conversation with the young woman at the front desk. When I felt it was safe to do so, I asked her if anything unusual had ever taken place in the old structure. Without hesitation, she affirmed my suspicions. Then she handed me a sheet of paper giving a brief history of the place. Sure enough, about three paragraphs down, there was a blurb about the ghost of Alma Matthews and how she was still hanging around the place, looking over those who chose to take up lodgings there.

After supper, I returned to the hostelry. The front desk was now commanded by a young man working his way through seminary. I told him of my experiences up on the fourth floor, and he offered to take me on a tour of the place, showing me where others had encountered dear old Alma. As we descended into the basement, he said,

> This is a really weird part of the building. About three weeks ago, we were having trouble with some plumbing, and we called in the servicemen. Two of them went down here to check things out, and after about fifteen minutes they came up again. I asked if they were finished, and they said they weren't. They told me they were taking a coffee break until the woman down there went away. When I asked what woman they were

talking about, they said there was an old woman who suddenly appeared from out of nowhere and watched them work. I guess she stayed across the room from them, over in a corner where there wasn't any doorway. Whenever they'd look over toward where she was, well, sometimes she'd be there and sometimes she wouldn't. They were a bit unsettled about it, but not really scared bad—they said New York is like that and they had worked in haunted places before.

Our tour continued through the basement, over the main floor, and up the stairs to each individual floor above. On the third floor, just as we were approaching the open door leading to the hallway, the doorstop suddenly flew out from underneath the door and down the hallway about ten feet or so, and the door slammed shut before us. My host just said, "No problem, it's just Alma. She won't bother you, but she likes to let people know she's around."

I spoke the next morning with a colleague of mine who had flown in from out of state for the series of mundane meetings we were to attend. Over pancakes and eggs he commented on how strange the accommodations were. I flat out told him I had encountered a ghost, and he gave me a wry sort of grin. "Me, too," he said. "Don't tell anyone this," he continued,

> but last night I woke up around 2 A.M. to use the bathroom down the hall. When I came back to my room, I discovered I had left my keys in my pants pocket and the door was locked. I didn't much feel like heading downstairs in just my tightie whities to get a spare key from the night clerk, but I thought I had no choice. Just as I started walking away from my room, I heard the knob turn and the door swung open.

My friend tells me he had to choose whether to go back in his room with an unseen guest or sleep on the sofa on the main floor. Since he only had on his underwear, modesty opted for the ghost. Strange thing, modesty.

I've not had the opportunity to go back to Greenwich

Village lately, although I'd love to do so. The clerk on duty the morning I left wouldn't have any conversation with me about the ghost of old Alma, insisting the blurb in the hotel literature about her roaming the old quarters was just a gag. He's not fooling me.

22

These Ghosts
Are Everywhere

Location of Haunting: Tombstone sits peacefully in the extreme southeastern corner of Arizona. It is only about thirty minutes by car from there to Mexico. Want to go? Buy a map, get a plane ticket, and enjoy.

Period of Haunting: Begun as a silver mining community in the 1870s, Tombstone appears to have been haunted by its unfortunate dead since its earliest days. It is still considerably haunted—perhaps the city most overrun with restless ghosts of all I've visited. It is not unusual at all for visitors to encounter the ghosts, as it appears most of the historic buildings are home to several. If you love ghosts, you can't avoid Tombstone.

Date of Investigation: Summer of 2001.

Description of Location: Tombstone, Arizona, was founded when an adventurous soul decided to wander out into the middle of Indian territory and risk life and limb in pursuit of silver. He was told that all he would find there would be his tombstone. So, when he struck massive veins of precious metal and the town was born, he dubbed it "Tombstone."

Had it not been for the famous and notorious characters who resided from time to time in that fair city, Tombstone would have disappeared when the mines flooded in the late 1800s, washing away any further dreams of extracting riches from the bowels of the earth. Instead, Wyatt Earp, his brothers, and Doc Holliday blew the McLaury boys and Billy Clanton full of holes near the OK Corral, supplying the lifeblood needed to ensure that Tombstone would be the town too tough to ever die.

Much of the town is preserved to look the way it did back in the days when shady gamblers, amoral lawmen, assorted badmen, and loose women all plied their trade there. Many of the residents don period duds, and the main street comes to life every night. Music permeates the air as it rushes out the saloon doors, and everyone has a good time as they retreat to the glory days of long ago. It is a fun place to visit, and one where the entire family can have a wonderful time.

The Haunt Meter: * * * *

Since I was a little tyke, adorned with hat, chaps, and cap pistol, I always dreamed of visiting Tombstone, where legendary western figures stalked their prey and shot it out to the death on the dusty streets. In the summer of 2001, I finally had the chance to go.

I was visiting my eldest son, Rob, in New Mexico, when on the spur of the moment we threw a change of clothes in the trunk of his Mazda and tooled off to the south through the Arizona mountains to the history-rich streets of Tombstone. Arriving just about supper time, we hurriedly checked into a nearby motel and scrambled on into town for the evening.

Everywhere I go, I find a creative way to bring up the subject of ghosts and hauntings and how I record stories about haunted spots, both public and private. Sitting in Big Nose Kate's Saloon, the topic came as second nature. The saloon girl I spoke with—I'll call her Sadie, because in truth I can't recall her real name and because Sadie is a good old western gal's name—proved to be a wealth of information about the ghostly doings of her famous town.

Sadie, decked out in dance-hall garb, parked herself down at our table after serving us generous helpings of appropriate libations. "What do you want to know?" she asked. "Or should I say, where do you want me to start?" I found that to be a most intriguing opening remark, so I asked her to just jump in and start running.

"I've been working here a few years," said Sadie,

and I can tell you with absolute certainty that Big Nose Kate's is full of ghosts. Just last week our bartender was busy serving tourists and the bar was pretty full. He asked one lone customer what he wanted, filled a mug with beer from the tap right there and looked up only to find the man gone. He was fascinated by it and told me about it later. When he described the guy, he fit the description of a ghost I call Pete, who's been seen around here by a lot of people. Pete always shows up wearing a striped shirt, button trousers, suspenders, and a sombrero. That's not really unusual around here though, because a lot of the locals dress that way. Pete sort of blends in.

(Blends in? There's a vivid thought.)

When I asked if old Pete has ever been spotted by the customers, she assured me that he had.

One afternoon late in the year, we were really busy, and this guy went to the back of the saloon to use the men's room. While he was in there, he said this man wearing a cowboy outfit strode through the door, walked behind him and over to the sink. When the customer spoke to him, he said the guy just peered over at him and disappeared. The man was pretty shook up, but his description sounded like old Pete to me. There's really nothing to be afraid of, because Pete's just sort of attached to the place and never causes anyone any harm.

I asked Sadie to show me the most haunted areas of the establishment, and she said the ghosts are plentiful and that they generally roam around all over the place.

"Once," she says,

> I was coming out of the back room after getting some
> supplies for the bar. To get from the back room to the
> main saloon area you have to turn and go through a
> narrow opening between the wall and the end of the
> bar. It's a tight squeeze if you're carrying things. As I
> turned to go through that passageway I felt someone
> grab my rear end real firm-like and squeeze it. I
> thought someone had come up from behind me and
> was getting a little too personal, but when I swung
> around, no one was there. Since then, it's happened
> several more times to me and to other girls, too. We
> figure it's one of the old-time cowboys, up to the tricks
> he used when he frequented the place way back when.

Sadie introduced me to the manager of the watering
hole, who congenially invited me back to his office, a
cramped room relegated to the confines of the rear of
the building. There he showed me a plethora of photographs sent to him from various tourists over the
years. All of them were snapshots of ghosts, sometimes
just mysterious orbs or cloudy, white forms and sometimes images of people who have entered the photos
without proper invitation. He says he receives at least
one such photo every week, and that the ghosts at Big
Nose Kate's are always prowling about. He told me if I
wanted to see the most heavily haunted area of the
saloon, he would have Sadie escort me down to the
basement.

The basement area sports three sectioned-off rooms.
The middle room is a western wear shop, the room off to
the right is for storage purposes and not often fre-
quented, and in the room to the left, barred from public
use, is a passageway leading to an underground tunnel.
The tunnel twists and turns until it ends at an old silver
mine. Long ago, miners put the entries to their mines
inside stores to keep just anyone from wandering in and
making a claim on their silver. The room with the tunnel
entrance was once used by an owner of this particular

mine, and his bed and some of his belongings are still in plain view. Incidentally, he was stabbed to death on that bed, and it is said that his ghost frequently shows up on photographs taken in that area.

The western wear shop is busiest of them all as far as ghostly activity is concerned. Sadie asked me to wander around a bit and see if I could sense anything strange. I had no confidence that I would, since I don't seem to be tuned in to the flavor of paranormal presences. However, as I strolled past the rear corner of the shop, I stepped into an icy cold patch of air and then back out again. When I admitted this to Sadie, she smiled and said, "That's where a love-struck woman hung herself when her cowboy boyfriend dumped her for another woman—way back in the 1880s."

Another little ditty was offered for my edification. Sadie pointed out an area up on the main floor of the saloon where a hangman's noose hangs from the ceiling. There's a small scaffold underneath that noose, and tourists step right up, place the noose around their neck, and have their photograph taken. For authenticity, they can pay a small fee and dress up in clothing of yesteryear, and one of the employees of the establishment will play the part of hangman. "More than once," says Sadie,

> a tourist has put on the clothes and paid for a lynching photo, and then had the rope around their neck suddenly tighten, as though it was tugged by unseen hands. It's always just playful, and no one has ever been hurt, but it scares the daylights out of them.

Sadie is purported to be psychic by nearly everyone who knows her. I asked her if she thought she could contact a ghost for me and get it to consent to having its picture taken. She willingly took me into the back storeroom where she claims the ghosts enjoy hanging out and, amid the stacks of beer cans and junk food, she went into a state of deep concentration. "They're here," she said, "all around us, but they're a little skittish about showing themselves because they don't know you." I snapped a few shots anyway, in hopes of catching a spirit or two in the act of haunting the place, but to no avail.

The next day my son and I once again toured the streets of Tombstone. We visited the building that used to be the Oriental Saloon, where Wyatt Earp did his thing at the gambling tables, and which hosted its fair share of gunfights. It is a clothing store. While talking with the proprietor about hauntings (everyone in Tombstone speaks freely of the ghosts), the clothes rack next to us began to spin around. It's supposed to do that, but only if someone is purposefully scanning the merchandise. In our case, no one was even near the rack. "See," said the owner, "this kind of stuff happens all the time."

Our next stop was the Bird Cage Saloon, an old-time bar and dance hall on the edge of the main business district. This is where all the action was back in the rough old days. It still sports the original furnishings of the day, right down to the poker chips on the tables. Nothing has changed inside since the day it was abandoned in the late 1880s. The ghosts there are legendary and have been written up in more books than I care to name here. I took the nickel tour and, interesting as it was, I never caught a fleeting glimpse of anything unusual.

23

The River Ghost

Location of Haunting: Located near a West Virgina mountain community called Bruceton Mills, there is no established address for this haunted site, as it is an open field near a river, which in turn flows by a cattle farm. It seems this is one of those locations where local young people like to gather for bonfires, beer parties, and late-night shenanigans.

Period of Haunting: According to those interviewed, the legend of this haunting goes back several decades, but many things have been experienced recently.

Date of Investigation: The information gathered for this story came to me during a visit to the Holiday Inn on Saratoga Avenue in Morgantown, West Virginia. I was enjoying a late-evening sandwich and beverage, when I struck up a conversation with the man behind the bar. He insisted on authenticating his story by calling over some of his friends who had also come face-to-face with weird experiences while cavorting in that otherwise pastoral setting.

Description of Location: Bruceton Mills is a large enough town to show up in my road atlas, but small enough of a settlement not to be listed in the index where the population figures are normally given. Suffice it to say, it really does exist "out there" in the rolling West Virginia hill country, and there are signs along I-68 letting you know when you're approaching the right (and I believe, only) exit. To get on with things, simply follow these not so simple directions, passed on from bartender to ghosthunter. Travel east on I-68, keeping a watch for the Bruceton Mills exit. At the end of the exit ramp, turn right and travel an additional two miles until you reach Little Sandy Creek and again turn right. The road then splits, so you will need to veer to the right yet again. Eventually, the pavement turns into dirt, passing a cattle farm and supposedly taking you to a beautiful river with an enchanting little waterfall. Although I verified these directions with the amiable dispenser of liquid spirits and his somewhat sober associates, travel the route at your own risk. I did not attempt a jaunt to this tranquil locale, opting out of a nocturnal visit down unfamiliar dirt roads where the owner of that cattle farm may be less than enthusiastic about out-of-state plates skirting his property. I am not so put off by ghosts as I am by the thought of viewing a West Virginia double-barreled shotgun from the receiving end. If any dear reader develops the burning inclination to check this place out, I would suggest doing so in the daylight hours, as the real fright just might be getting lost in some very rural country setting. If you have trouble finding your way and need directions better than those I've supplied herein, drive back to Morgantown to the Holiday Inn on Saratoga Avenue and ask the bartender, a friendly chap by the name of Lakin, to guide you onto the straight and narrow.

The Haunt Meter: * * ½

West Virginia is an interesting place to visit, or even to simply drive through on the way to someplace else. That's exactly what I was doing—traversing my way to Oakland, Maryland—when I decided my eyelids were heavy enough to warrant a night at the Morgantown Holiday Inn. After checking into my room and freshening up a tad, my stomach needed some attention, and that's what brought me to the bar and my acquaintance with Lakin (yes, it's his real name, even I couldn't make this one up).

Barroom chit-chat is a genre all to itself, so it wasn't difficult at all to introduce myself and expound a bit on what brought me to this part of the country. I've discovered that when folks learn you check out and write about haunted places, they either cut the conversation short and not-so-sweet, or buy you another round and regale you with their personal tales of haunted moments. The latter was the case in this upscale watering hole.

After a quick spiel about some of my experiences checking out haunted places, my friendly mixologist asked me in turn if I had ever had the opportunity to visit the so-called haunted river of Bruceton Mills. World traveler that I am, I still had to admit I had never heard of the local ghostly swimming hole. Not a bit dissuaded by my regional ignorance, Lakin went on the fill me in. "I've been there a few times myself," he said. "You know, it's a good place to party, to swim, and drink beer. The girls love it because no matter what they say, they like to be scared."

It appears the legend surrounding this secluded spot is so old that no one really knows, or even has an idea, why it's a haunted place. The best I can find out is that "someone must have died out there," which is a common way a place gets haunted. Speculation has it that someone—or a few someones—drowned many moons ago while dipping in the rippling waters, or that the haunting may be the result of a dead soldier or two still hanging around long after the close of the Civil War, even though there's no indication there was ever any skirmishes in that general vicinity.

"It was kind of strange a couple of times when I was up there with friends," says Lakin.

We'd gone up with a couple cases of beer and some firewood 'cause it's a great place to camp out or just party with friends. I remember once when we were camping out there and one of my buddies woke me up, probably around 4 A.M. I could tell he was scared, and he whispered for me to be quiet and listen, so I did. After a couple seconds, I could hear what sounded like a woman crying off over by the riverbank.

Lakin went on to say that the crying lasted for several minutes, and at times it seemed pretty mournful. "We just listened, and pretty soon it just stopped. Neither one of us were in a hurry to see what was going on out there. Maybe we would have if we hadn't already heard the place was haunted."

It appears the nocturnal weeping is not the only activity taking place out in the hill country of northern West Virginia. Several persons have reportedly witnessed white forms drifting along the riverbanks, and on some occasions the ghosts seem to take on more than a misty form. After listening to Lakin spin his tale for a while, I was encouraged about his story having some credibility when he called two of his friends over from their perch in the rear of the bar, where they had been entranced by stock car footage on television and hadn't heard our conversation at all. Lakin introduced me and asked them to tell me about the haunted river out by Bruceton Mills. They repeated similar stories and personal experiences.

So, if you ever find yourself passing through Morgantown on the way to someplace else, take a chance, if you dare, and give my directions a try. Maybe you'll actually stumble across this interesting little nightspot. If you get lost, well, you're on your own.

Index

People and Places

11th Street (New York City), 209
14th Street (Escanaba), 78

A

Albion College, 37, 42, 43
Allegan County, 171
Alma Matthews House, 209–214
American Society for Psychical Research, 195
Andy (the cat), 172
Anjanette, vii–xi
Ann Arbor, 4, 133, 191–192
Annie, 21–23
Argentine Road (Byron), 4
Arizona, 215–220
Auburn, 151
Austin Road (Manchester), 134
Automobile Hall of Fame, 152

B

B., Brenda, 105–106
B., Ken, 105–106
Barton Street (Garden City), 153
Bay City, 152
Beckwith Theatre, 67–76
Beckwith Theatre Company, 67
Jennie (actress), 75

Becky, 135–142
Berrien Street (Albion), 36
Big Nose Kate's Saloon, 216–220
Bird Cage Saloon, 220
Blackhawks, 107
"Blanche", 2, 88–90, 92–93, 98, 99, 100
Bock, C.E., 55, 62
Bos, Tim, 85–87, 90–95, 96, 97–98, 100
Bruceton Mills, 221–224
Brynner, Yul, 106
Buckner, Garrett, 79
Buckner, Lana, 79–81
Tina (psychic), 81–83
Buckner, Lucy, 79–81
Buddy's Pizza, 20
Buford, 203
Bush, Pam, 87–89, 90
Byron, 3–4, 7–17

C

Caro, xiv
Chelsea, 78
Cherry Hill (Dearborn), 19
Chicago, 52
Christmas Tree farm, 143–150
Civil War, 86, 95, 134, 192, 201–207, 223
Clanton, Billy, 216
Clay Stokes Agency, 167
Clinton, Bill, 192
Clover, Bernice, 108–112

Clover, Clarence, 108–112
Cofer-Jones, Melissa, 47–48
Coloma High School Library, 52
Commerce Road (Milford), 166
Confederacy, 204
Crandall, Jody, 52
Creger, Father Stanley, 39
Creston Avenue (Westland), 185
Cutcher, Brett, 8–9
Cutcher, Flo, 3–15
    Mary (Flo's mother) 4–7
Cutcher, Stefanie, 8, 11–16
Cutcher, Ted, 7–9

D

Dairy Queen, 34, 134
Daniels, Jeff, 78, 101
Dearborn, 19–23
Dearborn Heights, 25–50
Decatur, 51
Delta County, 78
DeMille, Cecil B., 106
Depot Town, 192
Detroit, xiv, 19, 52, 114, 144, 152, 185, 191
"Devil's Den", 203
Devon, 119
Dew Drop Inn, 78
Dowagiac, 51–66, 67–76
Dow Chemical Company, 152
Dow Historical Museum, Herbert H., 152
Dunhill Road (Byron), 4

E

Earp, Wyatt, 215, 220

East Lansing, xv, 107
Eastern Michigan University, 192
Edison, Thomas, 19
Edwards, John, 190
Eloise (mental hospital), 187–188
Emily, 144–147, 149–150
Escanaba, 77–83, 177–178
Escanaba in da Moonlight, 78
Eugene (the cat), 172–176

F

Fairlane (Henry Ford Estate), 19
Fenton, 4–7
Flint, 151
Ford, Henry, 19
Ford Motor Company, The, 19
Ford Museum, Henry, 19
Ford Road (Garden City), 153
Forest Highway 5230, 178
Front Street (Dowagiac), 51, 56
"Fudge Island". *See* Mackinac Island

G

Gable, Clark, 106
Galen, 135–142
Garden City, 153
Gayle, 119–121
Gettysburg Battlefield, *199*, 201 207
Gettysburg Pennsylvania, 201–207
"ghost lights", 179–183

Ginger, 154–163
Gladstone, 78, 177
Godfather, The, 105
Gone With the Wind, 106
Grace, 166–170
Grand Hotel, The, 126
Grand Rapids, xvi
"Grandma", 185–190
Greenfield Village, 19
Greenwich Village, 209–214
Grove Street (Midland), 151, 154
Gunn, Jeff, 62–64
Gwynn, Ernie, 126–131
Gwynn, Lydia, 126–131

H

Haley Street (Midland), 151
Hartland Road (Fenton), 4
Haunt Meter, xxiii
"Heck", 110
Heller, Joseph, 52
Henry Ford Estate, 19
Henry Ford Museum, 19
Herbert H. Dow Historical Museum, 19
Heston, Charlton, 106
Highway 2, 125
Highway 31, 51
Highway 45, 178
Highway 51, 51
Holcomb, Dutch, 185–190
Holcomb, Sandi, 185–190
Holliday, Doc, 215
Howell, 7
Hudon, Lori, 172–176
Hudon, Michael, 172–176
Hunter, Grandma, 153
Hunter, Rev. Gerald, *148*
Hunter, Rob, 179–180, 216

Hunter, Tracey, 203–207

I

I-68, 221
I-75, 125, 151–152
I-94, 51, 103, 107, 133, 172
Ignacio-Gunn, Lacy, 56–66, 67–76
Ignacio, John, 57–58, 63–64
Indiana Turnpike, 51
Inkster, 185

J

Jackson, 85–100, 101–106, 107, 133, 135
Jackson Antique Mall, 2, *84*, 85–100
Nina (employee), 88–89
Jackson Street (Jackson), 85
Joe, 166–170

K

Kalamazoo, 171
Karloff, Boris, 153–154
Kennedy, Cybil, 26, 31, 35–36
Kennedy, Devon, 26, 30
Kennedy Family, 25–50
Kristen (psychic consulted), 49–50
Kennedy, Kaitlynn, 26–47
Brendan (Kaitlynn's boyfriend), 39, 43
Kennedy, Kerry, 26–29, 32–33, 36, 41
Kennedy, Mary, 26, 41

Kennedy, Stacey, 26, 28–29
Keweenaw Peninsula, 179
Knights of Columbus Hall, 67
Kresge, Bonnie, 85–86, 90–94, 97–98
Kroger, 188

L

LaGuardia Airport, 209
Lake Huron, 125–126
Lake Michigan, 126
Lake Superior, 178
Lakin (West Virginia bartender), 222–224
Lansing, 107
Laurel Park Mall, 114
Lee, Gen. Robert E., 203
Leigh, Vivien, 106
Leslie, 107–112, 191, 196
Lewis, Eleanor, 87–90
Lininger, Edgar, 21–23
Little Bay de Noc, 78
Little Sandy Creek, 222
"Little Round Top", 203
Livonia, 113–123, 185
Log Cabin Supper Club, 78
Longstreet, Gen. James, 203
Lower Peninsula, 125, 143–150, 177
Ludington Park, 79
Ludington Street, 77–79

M

M-52, 133
M-59, 4,166
Mackinac Bridge, 78, 126, 177–178
Mackinac City, 125, 130
Mackinac Island, 125–131
Main Street (Mackinac Island), 126
Main Street (Milford), 166
Manchester, 133–142
Manchester Cemetery, *132*, 133–142
Manistique, 177
Mark, 154–163
Marquette, xvi–xvii, 178–179
Martin High School, 172
Maryland, 201
Matthews, Alma, 209–214
Matthews House, Alma, 209–214
Maryland, 221–224
McDonald's, 151
McKenzie, Karla, 114–123
McKenzie, Tom, 114–123
McLaury boys, 216
Mead Paper Company, 78
Meade, Gen. George, 203
Mechanic Street (Jackson), 101
Meijer's, 114
Merriman Street (Garden City), 153
Mexico, 215
Michigan Avenue (Jackson), 103
Michigan Forest Service, 180
Michigan Normal School, 192
Michigan State Spartans, 107
Michigan Theatre, 85, 101–106, *102*
Mid-Michigan, 196
Midland, 151–163
Midland Mall, 152
Mighty Mac, 177
Milford, 165–170
Milford Road (Milford), 166
"Mr. Bock", *see* Bock, C.E.

Mitchell, Margaret, 106
Morgantown, West Virginia, 221–224
Mt. Pleasant, 152
Munising, 178
Myers, Doug, 144–147, 149–150
Myers, Susan, 144–147, 149–150

N

Napoleon street (Manchester), 134
National Park Service, 201
New Baltimore, xiv
New Mexico, 216
New York, New York, 209–214
Northern Lights, 179
Northern Michigan University, 178
Northview Cemetery, 19–23
Norvell, 136

O

Oakland County, 165
Oakland, Maryland, 222
Oakwood Drive (Byron), 3–17
Ohio, 196
OK Corral, 216
Old Sauk Trail, 191
Olympia Bookstore, 51–56, 67, 68
Osis, Karliss, 195
Otsego, 171–176
Ouija boards, 65, 72–73, 136
Outer Drive (Dearborn), 19

P

Paulding, 177–183
"Peach Orchard, The", 203
Pearl Street (Jackson), 85, 92
Pennsylvania, 201–207
"Pete" (ghost), 217
Pickett, Gen. George E., 203–204
Pickett's Charge, 203–204
Pictured Rocks National Lakeshore, 178
Porcupine Mountains, 179
Pugh, Paul, 51–56, 67, 68

R

Radio Shack, 137
Redford, xv–xvi
Reese, xiii
Reynolds, General, 203–204
Ridge, Allison, 20–23
    Martin (Allison's boyfriend), 20–21
Ripley's Believe It or Not, 180
Robbins Pond, 177–183
Robbins Pond Road (Paulding), 178
Route 89, 171
Royal Oak, xv

S

Sadie, 216–220
schoolhouse, haunted, vii–xi
Saginaw, 152, 154
St. Francis Hospital, 77–83
St. Ignace, 177
St. Mary's Hospital, 113

Sanford, 158
Saratoga Avenue
   (Morgantown, WV), 221–222
Sauk Indian Trail, 191
Sayklly's Confectionery, 177
Sherman, Gen. William
   Tecumseh, 95
Silver Lake Road (Byron), 4
Simpson, Homer, 65
Sisters of St. Francis, 77
Sleepy Hollow Road, 178
Smith, Kay, 55
Steven's Point, Wisconsin, 79
"The Stomper", 90
Stone, Jake, 104
Stone, Katie, 103–105
Super Sucker, 101
Susan, 192–197

T

Telegraph Road (Dearborn
   Heights), 26
Ten Commandments, The, 106
Terrace Motor Inn, 78
Tittabawassee River, 152
Tombstone, Arizona, 215–220
Tom's (restaurant), 103
Traverse City, xiv
"Tridge", 152

U

Union Soldier statue, *132*,
   133–134
University of Michigan, 192
Upper Peninsula, 77–78, 125,
   177
US-10, 151

US-12, 26, 51, 191
US-127, 103, 107
US-131, 171
US-2, 177–178
US-23, 4
US-28, 178
US-77, 178

V

Vonnegut, Kurt, 52

W

WaldenBooks, 107
Wampler's Lake, 117
Watersmeet, 178
Wayne, 185
West Virginia, 221–224
Western Michigan Ghost
   Hunters Society, 4
Westland, 185–190
Westwood Mall, 107
Wheeler, Suki, 2, 98–99
Wisconsin, 178
Wolf Lake, 136
Wooster, Ohio, 196
Wright Brothers, 19

Y

"Yooper", 77–78
Ypsilanti, 191–197

Gerald S. Hunter

Gerald S. Hunter is an ordained United Methodist minister currently serving a parish church in mid-Michigan. He was educated at Albion College, where he received a Bachelor of Arts degree in Religious Studies, and at The Methodist Theological School in Ohio, where he received a Master of Divinity degree. Rev. Hunter is currently enrolled in the Master of Counseling program at Central Michigan University in Mount Pleasant.

An avid writer, Rev. Hunter has had articles published in *The Detroit Free Press*, *The Akron Beacon Journal*, and *The Michigan Christian Advocate*. He has also taught creative and business writing at Saginaw Valley State University as an adjunct instructor of English.

Rev. Hunter and his wife, Tracey, maintain a home in Hillsdale County, Michigan.

Publisher's Credits

Cover design by Timothy Kocher. Interior design by Sharon Woodhouse. Layout by Ken Woodhouse and Sharon Woodhouse. Photos by Gerald Hunter. Drawings by Suki Wheeler. Editing by Mary McNulty. Proofreading by Sharon Woodhouse, Karen Formanski, and Ken Woodhouse. Index by Karen Formanski and Ken Woodhouse. The text of *More Haunted Michigan* was set in Bookman Old Style, with heads in Zanders.

Notice

Haunted?

If you would like to share your own haunted Michigan experiences with Rev. Hunter, you may contact him by mail at Thunder Bay Press; 2325 Jarco Drive; Holt, MI 48842. We request that you respect Rev. Hunter's privacy and refrain from attempting to reach him at his home or work.

More Ghost Stories

Haunted Michigan: Recent Encounters with Active Spirits
by Rev. Gerald S. Hunter
In his tour of the two peninsulas, Rev. Hunter doesn't recount legends or the spooky events of long ago, but active hauntings that continue to this day. Join his investigations into the modern-day ghost stories and open your mind to the presence of the paranormal all around us. Called a "compelling collection of modern ghost stories" by the Midwest Book Review.
1-933272-00-7, $12.95

Haunted Indiana
by Mark Marimen
As the slogan goes, "There's more than corn in Indiana." If the ghostly legends and tales that can be heard are to be believed, indeed there is more than corn in the Hoosier state – restless spirits that refuse to stay buried and forgotten. Come visit *Haunted Indiana*, the first in a series of four ghostly books by Mark Marimen. Also available: *Haunted Indiana 2, 3, and 4.*
1-882376-38-2, $13.95

Chicagoland Ghosts
by Dylan Clearfield
The singing ghost of Joliet Prison, phantom monks at St. Rita's Church, ghostly gunfire from the site of the St. Valentine's Day massacre, and the ghost of Clarence Darrow, these are just a few of Chicagoland's amazing ghosts. You will find these and many more is this long-awaited book. Also available: *Floridaland Ghosts.*
1-882376-41-2, $12.95

Michigan Ghost Towns of the Upper Peninsula
by R. L. Dodge
This guide to long forgotten ghost towns relates an accurate history of hundreds of areas in the Upper Peninsula of which little or nothing has ever been written about in books. Also available: *Michigan Ghost Towns of the Lower Peninsula.*
0-934884-02-1, $15.95

More Ghost Stories

Haunts of the Upper Great Lakes
by Dixie Franklin
A bit of superstition haunts most of us– a remnant perhaps of the
memories of chillingly scary ghost stories told to us in our childhood. Northen Wisconsin and Michigan's Upper Peninsula have
more than their share of ghosts and haunted places. There are
haunted lighthouses, haunted mansions and inns, and haunted
woods– all waiting for you in *Haunts of the Upper Great Lakes.*
1-882376-47-1, $13.95

Michigan Haunts and Hauntings
by Marion Kuclo, "Gundella"
This colletion of Gundella's favorite tales and ghost stories from
and about the region– Indian legends, folklore from Michigan's
early days as a territory, and modern-day hauntings– is presented with her special blend of story-telling and research.
1-882376-00-5, $11.95

Ghosts Towns of Michigan
by Larry Wakefield
Here is the first volume in the *Ghost Towns of Michigan* series,
featuring thirty-three of Michigan's most fascinating ghost towns,
along with numerous historic photographs. These are stories of
land speculators, wildcat bankers, boom-and-bust lumber bar-
ons, pioneers who refused to give up, and small towns with big
ideas that didn't quite pan out. Also available: *Ghost Towns of
Michigan Volume 2 and 3.*
1-882376-77-3, $15.95

Ghosts of the Great Lakes: More Than Mere Legend
by Megan Long
The Great Lakes have a colorful past that spans hundreds of
years, stretches over thousands of miles... and sometimes crosses into the spirit world. *Ghosts of the Great Lakes* takes readers
from the far eastern shores of Lake Ontario to western Lake Superior, revealing haunting and strange tales.
1-882376-89-7, $17.95

Other Titles from Thunder Bay Press

Bunyan & Banjoes:
Michigan Songs and Stories
Kitty Donohoe
Book: 1882376285, $10.95
Book & CD: 1882376587, $19.95

Charlotte Avery on Isle Royale
Rebecca S. Curtis
1882376900, $9.95

Farewell to the Island
Gloria Whelan
1882376927, $7.95

Great Lakes Indians
William J. Kubiak
1882376854, $14.99

Mystery on Mackinac Island
Anna W. Hale
188237648X, $10.95

Sisu
Sue Harrison
Hardcover: 1882376404, $16.95
Paperback: 1882376390, $11.95

Outlaws of the Lakes
Edward Butts
1882376919, $17.95

Michigan Rogues, Desperados
& Cut-Throats
Tom Powers
1882376862, $12.95

Canoeing Michigan Rivers
Jerry Dennis & Craig Date
1882376951, $16.95

Kitchen Table Bird Book
John Ham & David Mohrhardt
1882376153, $15.95

Michigan Wildflowers
Harry C. Lund
1882376560, $18.95

Michigan's Best Campgrounds
Jim DuFresne
1933272031, $16.95

All Hell Broke Loose
William H. Hull
188237696X, $12.95

Disaster Great Lakes
Megan Long
1882376889, $19.95

Michigan On Fire
Betty Sodders
1882376528, $19.95

Shipwrecks of the Great Lakes
Paul Hancock
1882376846, $19.95

Deadly Waters
Christopher H. Meehan
080284068X, $8.00